Out of Focus...*Again*

A JOURNEY FROM **DEPRESSION** TO **RECOVERY**
THROUGH COURAGE, LOVE AND COMMITMENT

Ann Kochenberger

Morgan James Publishing • New York

Out of Focus...Again

A Journey from Depression to Recovery Through Courage, Love and Commitment

Library of Congress Control Number: 2008924952
ISBN: 978-1-60037-444-9   (Paperback)

PUBLISHED BY:

Morgan James Publishing, LLC
1225 Franklin Ave Ste 325
Garden City, NY 11530-1693
Toll Free 800-485-4943
www.MorganJamesPublishing.com

www.morganjamespublishing.com

Habitat for Humanity®
Peninsula
Building Partner

GENERAL EDITOR:
Heather Campbell

COVER & INTERIOR DESIGN BY:
3 Dog Design
www.3dogdesign.net
chris@3dogdesign.net

*To Gary, who insisted I stay
and to Susan and Dave, the reasons I did*

Table of Contents

Testimonials

"I have been honored by Ann to be have been her first psychotherapist on this journey she has so honestly and eloquently portrayed in *Out of Focus...Again*. It is my hope that all readers will find enlightenment, understanding, empathy and, ultimately, hopefulness, whether the battle with depression has challenged themselves, a family member or a friend."

Dr. David A. (Sandy) Macdonald, PhD

* * * *

"Ann takes us on her journey that winds its way through pain and suffering, love and triumph. Her travels have many stops that are shared by those close to her who, through their caring and their actions, help her map the way to health and well-being. *Out of Focus...Again* is an important book for those who think they must take the journey alone and that others will not understand. Ann lives to help others and this book continues that legacy."

Rick Jacobs, PhD, Professor of Psychology, Penn State University

* * * *

"In reading *Out Of Focus...Again* I realized how fortunate Ann was and is to have a very loving and supportive family. She made some excellent decisions by learning to say "no", taking care of herself, and putting family first. Ann also knows that because she has bi-polar disorder, she needs to do so without guilt. Honest, compelling, and well-written are good descriptive adjectives for this book."

Rosemarie Mc Dermott, lifelong friend

* * * *

"WOW ... Ann's incredibly focused, out of focus and refocused journey through the maze of depression is a must read for anyone diagnosed with this debilitating illness. Make sure that family members and loved ones get a copy too."

Judith Briles, The Confidence Factor

"Written from the heart of someone who is aware of the perils of depression firsthand. If a resource such as *Out of Focus...Again* had been there for Ann and our family, all of us would have benefited. This touching chronicle speaks to those who desperately need direction and hope...from someone who truly understands."

Fran Baker, family member

* * * *

"Ann Kochenberger has written a compelling account of her own depression and the relief she found through her determined pursuit of effective treatment. Those who suffer from depression will identify with what she has experienced and be encouraged in their efforts to recover. Those who have friends or loved ones who are depressed will learn about this common condition and the help that is available."

Jon Bell, M.D.

* * * *

"The book's stunning description of the reality of depression is one of the most compelling I have ever encountered. What makes it extraordinary is the author's ability to describe and integrate the personal, familial, and social context of her illness. There are few other treatments as authentic or comprehensive."

Frank J. Landy, PhD, Professor of Psychology

Acknowledgments

I would not be at the place I am today were it not for the unremitting love and support of my husband, Gary. His continuous encouragement, coupled with his seemingly infinite patience throughout each recovery process allowed me to have some semblance of hope.

My two children, Susan and Dave, whom I love more than life, enabled me some sense of sanity during the times I was in darkness. For me, the lure of freedom from mental anguish was not able to surpass that of a mother's love for her children.

My grandchildren Max, Anna, Morgan, Ben and Nina are highlights of my days. Their curiosities, love and laughter continually reinforce my many decisions to "get through the rain storm" to sunshine beyond.

I have a terrific son-in-law, John Stroeher, and a wonderful daughter-in-law, Kelly Kochenberger, both of whom I love very much. I thank them for being non-judgmental, patient and understanding.

A very special thanks to my sister, Susan Daniels, who has always been a part of my earliest memories because of our closeness in age; but also because of her love and devotion to me as a sister and best friend.

To my brother Ray Baker and my sister-in-law, Fran, who opened their home and hearts to me at a time when I was falling fast. Thanks also to Nick, Alex and Matt Baker who shared activities and friends and willingly became an important part of my "family" that year.

To Fran, who always made time. Notes on the coffee pot, invitations to ride with her to pick up Alex or Matt and her inclusion of me in all family outings were reminders of my importance to family.

To my three other siblings, Bill, Betsy and Bob who are among my closest friends. Thanks for the concern you have shown and the love you have always given.

With gratitude to my brother-in-law and "personal pharmacist," Dave Kochenberger, who has devoted much time throughout the years, guiding me when I considered medication changes and whose support and friendship have always been an important part of my life.

I know that many family members and friends would have willingly lent encouragement during bad days had they known the extent of my illness. To the few who did know, Jane Koot, Joan Fenton and my sister-in-law, Fran Baker, I am grateful for your love and support.

To those individuals who took time to read and edit throughout my writing process. Thanks to Barbara Reasoner for her creative ideas, and to Fran Baker, Margaret Moore and Marlene Smith for their input and, always, Gary.

The respect and admiration I hold for my main therapists, Dr. Sandy Macdonald, Carole Crawford and Dr. Jon Bell for their commitment to and belief in my recovery. The work that I did with each of them resulted in filling in some of the cracks of my psyche and gave me hope when I had very little.

Special thanks to Sandy Macdonald, with whom I had a professional relationship for more than a decade, and whose expertise has served me well.

To Mary Chapman, professional therapist and friend, who tirelessly devoted time to me when I lived in Mississippi, and again, after I moved to Denver. Her willingness and availability to talk through all of my options were what I needed at the time.

Dr. Judith Briles, my book shepherd, mentor and friend: Your belief in my ability as a writer and in the importance of the message I am sending to others, coupled with your willingness to mail my proposal and manuscript to various agents and publishers is the reason that *Out of Focus...Again* received the exposure that was needed.

My editor, Barbara Munson, is amazing. Her many suggestions each step of the way, along with her format creativity are much appreciated.

A parting thanks to my husband, Gary, whose enthusiasm over the first several pages I asked him to read years ago convinced me that I could write. I value the input he has provided, the many hours of proofreading he has done and the suggestions he has offered. As is true in our lives together, he has been beside me as I have written and rewritten *Out of Focus...Again*.

Foreword

BY

DAVID A. (SANDY) MACDONALD, PHD

STATE COLLEGE, PENNSYLVANIA

Depression, especially in its severest form so vividly chronicled in Ann's book, must be understood as the summation of a triad of genetic pre-disposition, personality style and life stressors converging to significantly shift one's mood, coping strategies and perception of one's life. For Ann, the outset appears to have been cataclysmic, without warning, without clear precursors, and without obvious trauma. The insidious process of rapid spiraling into emotional darkness was just as mysterious to her as the spontaneous and surprising uplifting of mood that offered brief respite and relief, only to have her plunge again into desperate and despairing confusion and depression.

There is no question that every experienced mental health professional has encountered persons suffering such as Ann, though each person is a unique convergence of the triad of factors that becomes the "signature" of his or her struggle. Some persons recall having always been depressed, although many locate a specific event, such as the death of a parent, as the trigger for the onset of their battle with depression.

As Ann takes us through her journey via journal entries and narrative, the reader will find the onset of her depression as confusing as it was for her. One can only surmise that there were powerful genetic elements that set the stage, coupled with her personal striving to be perfect in all her accomplishments whether playing tennis, running, parenting or teaching. Most poignantly, when her children became embroiled with some normal crises of growing up, Ann was extremely self-blaming for their less than perfect behavior. For many, these crises would not appear traumatic, but for Ann they were the final "tipping point" for her depression. The remissions, which arrived without forewarning, always carried with them a message of hopefulness in the unexpected reprieve they provided. The next sudden plunge into despair, equally unannounced by real-life events, gives a powerful picture of helplessness and the devastation of that very hopefulness she had relied upon to lift her spirits.

Fortunately for Ann, what might be considered the necessary elements for healing were there early on and throughout the course of her struggles to the present time. Those elements are those of a loving and supportive family, with her husband's patience, empathy and presence being at the core. This was coupled with early and persistent intervention with psychotherapy and psychiatric medication, both of which have become more sophisticated over the past thirty years. Finally, what could be considered the sufficient elements for the transformation of her life journey from depressively despairing to enthusiastically optimistic have been her personal fortitude, her courageous persistence, and, ultimately her indomitable spirit.

I have been honored by Ann to be have been her first psychotherapist on this journey she has so honestly and eloquently portrayed in *Out of Focus... Again*. I am particularly honored to have been asked to write this forward. It is my hope that all readers will find enlightenment, understanding, empathy and, ultimately, hopefulness, whether the battle with depression has challenged themselves, a family member or a friend.

Introduction

My name is Ann, and I am self-assured, outgoing and humorous. When depression is not present, I am articulate and my intelligence is apparent. I have tons of energy. I love every aspect of my life. Exercise, reading, walking my dog and writing bring me much joy. Having breakfast monthly with my son, Dave, and time with my daughter, Susan, are highlights of my life. I cherish my five grandchildren and spend time with them often.

I have been the best wife possible to my husband, Gary, whom I love with all my heart. Gary is easy-going and sensitive and also has a wonderful sense of humor. I admire him tremendously for his sense of ethics and his dedication to his profession. He is a great father and grandfather, and is loyal to his brothers and sisters as well as to all of our extended family. Best of all, he loves me.

We are both in the academic world. I earned a BS degree in history and elementary education from the University of Colorado in 1965. Gary went on to get a PhD in Business Administration after receiving a BS in electrical engineering and an MBA. I substitute taught when our children, Susan and Dave, were young; I then worked as a researcher and writer at Penn State once they were in school full time. Years later, when I returned to the classroom, I obtained a Masters in Education. I honestly loved going to work each day.

And when I hear the whir of the garage door opening each afternoon, I look forward to Gary's return and talking with him about our day. Before we go upstairs each evening, we sit down to a glass of wine or a cup of hot tea and further discuss what's on our minds.

But, in spite of the many blessings in my life, aside from the fact that I love my life and those with whom I share it, the darkness comes and goes. My days have been either wonderful or dreadful, unpredictably switching back and forth. It has been this way for more than thirty years.

* * *

I have never been able to adequately describe what it feels like to be depressed. I don't think it's possible. This illness is so many things. Sometimes many symptoms are present; other times, only a few. I might feel distraught, frustrated, anxious, self-defeated, guilty or scared. At times some of the feelings intensify until I think I am going to explode.

When depression is present, time is endless. Minutes seem like hours, hours like days; I think it's because the only place I am is inside my head. The world seems to continue on around me, but I am no longer a part of it. I am robotic; I have no feelings, no desires and no hopes.

But most of all, depression is darkness—a deep, black hole into which I have plunged. As I fall, the speed of the descent is amazingly rapid.

This depression controls me; I disappear, and a different person emerges. The person who takes my place is nothing like me. She has no name because giving her one would make her more of an entity. I don't want her to have more control over me than she has, so she remains nameless.

I dread her appearance, but am not able to prevent it. My replacement is weak. She is terrified. She is unable to put words together intelligently. I am not able to make her leave. I surrender because I have no other choice. The "real me" evaporates, gone in an instant.

My depression comes and goes, comes and goes. Each time it begins to reappear, the dominant feeling is that of defeat, made worse because I know what's coming.

My external world is out of focus, virtually a blur; I am not able to focus on it because of all that is going on inside. Thoughts and fears rush around in my brain, moving in haphazard ways, bumping into one another before they are thrust away as the result of the impact. Mixed among all the emotions are questions I hear, but before I think of an answer, another question emerges. I don't have time to think, and all of this creates panic...sheer panic. Anxiety is very much a part of my depression.

When I am experiencing depression, I awaken to a feeling of dread. A heavy sinking feeling tells me *it is back*. A weight presses on my chest; its pressure is so forceful that I can barely move. I am limp.

But I don't exist in a vacuum. When I am around people, I feel they are judging me. I am convinced that they believe I am incapable of doing anything worthwhile. I *know* they think I am a terrible mother, an incompetent teacher. I find that I have difficulty speaking intelligently. Searching for words, I stammer. My voice is unfamiliar, weak, tired. I can't wait to get away.

The pain is overwhelming, but it is a mental pain—at first. This pain inside my mind spreads throughout my body as my muscles ache, my arms tingle, my legs twitch. I become a person who can't think, eat, sleep or laugh. At its worst, I can't even cry. And then...I am no longer a person. I am just a useless body in incredible mental and physical anguish...and I want to die.

I am a wife, mother, grandmother, sister, teacher, and friend…and there have been many, many times that I have desperately wanted to take my own life.

IF YOU ARE DEPRESSED…

This book is meant for everyone who suffers from depression, but my first concern is for those who are thinking about suicide. Thoughts of suicide are all too common in people with severe depression. I know.

The second reason for my book is to give family members and friends an accurate picture of what we deal with every moment. By educating themselves, they will be better equipped to help or at least understand.

Most people think depression is a transient thing—when the problem goes away, so does the depression. That is true for some people. Severe depression, however, is a lifetime battle. Two general types exist: *Major depression* includes an array of symptoms that interfere with the ability to function normally. Work, sleep and appetite are all affected, resulting in a loss of pleasure. A major depression—which can last a few weeks, many months or, for some people, years—might occur only once in a lifetime but, more often, occurs several times.

Bipolar disorder is another common form of depression. Also called manic-depression, this type is not as prevalent, but can be just as debilitating. Characterized by mood swings of feeling high and low, those who are manic-depressive typically switch between being very depressed to feeling euphoric. These mood changes are usually gradual, but can be exaggerated and rapid.

If you or someone you love has depression—of any type—you will find help in this book. But I also want to emphasize the importance of seeking help from a mental health professional. This illness is not something that can *be* helped without help. It is *far* too complicated.

A JOURNAL SPRINGS TO LIFE

This book began as a journal. I bought my first one in 1974 at McLanahan's Drug Store on South Allen Street in State College, Pennsylvania. I vividly recall the notebook because it had a very unusual cover. Looking back, it is strange that I chose that particular one since I like bright colors and this cover was anything but. It had random lines crossing both horizontally and vertically. Where the lines intersected they formed geometric shapes against a black background. The triangles, circles and wavy lines were muted shades of gray, green and tan.

At that time I was doing a bit of what you might call "reflective writing" that conveyed my random thoughts. I had no symptoms of depression; they would begin to appear several months later, then disappear and reappear. At least I didn't *think* I was depressed, but perhaps my choice of a somber-covered journal was a subconscious preference, a premonition of what was yet to come.

My first entry in the journal is dated September 17, 1974. I recall that it was written as I sat looking out a window of Lemont Elementary School on a crisp, chilly day.

That journal would be the first of nine, kept over the years during times I was burdened with an illness all too common to millions. The pages contain entries indicating times of sadness, despair, guilt and frustration. The words describe fears, but also hope and determination. Carefully dated, each entry provides a glance into specific moments within specific days; they echo emotions held deep inside. My journal was my refuge, a safe haven where I could talk about the complications and the contradictions of my life. It was my private confidante, holding my secret thoughts from everyone else.

Thankfully, I never tossed out those first journals—they helped me recall the out of focus years as I wrote this book. I have included some of my journal entries here. Along with them, you will find "snapshots" of my other remembrances. These serve as illustrations of living with depression in real time. Through them, I hope you will have a better sense of what it was like for me.

The first two sections of the book contain my story, and all of the ways I desperately tried to help myself. Section III is a full description of all of my coping mechanisms accumulated over thirty years. They are listed in the order *in which they were most helpful* to me. I relied on every one of them. I hope they help you. You also will hear from Gary, my husband, and my children, Susan and Dave, throughout the book.

If you are under severe depression now and would like some immediate help, please skip over to Part III.

--Ann Kochenberger

Part 1

IMPERFECTIONS OF A PERFECT LIFE

CHAPTER 1:
Happy Birthday

SNAPSHOT : Pueblo, Colorado March 4, 1952

The presents are neatly arranged on the buffet, just like always. They are perfectly wrapped in bright yellow birthday paper and I wonder what is inside each one. I think I can see the pink dots of a Storybook doll through the thin paper of the gift on top.

I am ten years old today. The large mirror above the wrapped packages reflects freckles around a tiny nose, straight chin-length dark hair with bangs that could use a trim. The large silver tea service sparkles on a silver tray. My beautifully decorated birthday cake has been placed in front of it and it is topped with eleven candles—one for each year and "one to grow on."

Two sets of grandparents and Uncle Tim arrive for the celebration. After a special dinner, our fancy cake plates—stacked high—are placed next to the cake on the table. The lighted candles glow as I close my eyes to the musical sound of "Happy Birthday." I blow them all out in one breath as I secretly make a wish.

I remember making wishes like that when I was a little girl. I suppose I wished for something that was inside one of the brightly wrapped gifts. I didn't think to wish that my life would remain as it was at that moment—full of comfort, security...and happiness.

CHAPTER 2:
Gray Clouds Intermingled With Sunny Skies

JOURNAL ENTRY

State College, Pennsylvania Early September 1974

Autumn has arrived and, with it, signs of change...in early morning chill to colors that represent varying shades of me, my thoughts and reflections of past and present.

To lack moods is to never know oneself. Changes cause us to ponder reasons for existence, our desires, what is important to us and what is not.

I am like a leaf whose colors slowly change, each result bringing an inner growth and, sometimes, more of a balance, but sometimes not.

To experience emptiness and failure is to appreciate all that gives us joy and fulfillment. Sometimes I welcome solitude and, now and then, a touch of sadness.

I had been substitute teaching at Lemont School in State College, Pennsylvania the day I bought my first journal. I couldn't wait to write my first entry. My class was down the hall in art for an hour, so I sat alone in the teachers' lounge looking out the window. The leaves had begun to change, the colors varied on each tree, and I put pencil to notebook paper and started to write. I always loved what I wrote and was inspired to write often.

I must admit I was surprised at the words that sprang from my head, but I believed they were the creative result of delving into my innermost thoughts. Perhaps they were. I considered my writing an honest assessment of my view of the world and rather smugly thought it was indicative of my ability to truly understand what I was all about.

In retrospect, I think that all of the reflecting that was to follow was my way of rationalizing my burgeoning discontent. Unhappiness was beginning to slowly filter into my life. Denial was becoming my constant demon...perhaps because I could not believe I could be unhappy about anything.

* * *

The joy in which I exulted when I was a child continued throughout my young adult years. Married right out of high school, Gary and I wanted to pursue our college goals before we had children. Our first years together consisted mainly of studying, but we managed to have fun as well. After obtaining our bachelors degrees from the University of Colorado, Gary went on to graduate school and I taught first grade in Boulder for several years.

Our Susan arrived in October of 1966 and three years later—the last year of Gary's PhD program—we learned that Susan would have a sibling. About that time, Penn State University extended Gary a job offer. Accepting an assistant professor position, we eagerly embarked on a new chapter of our lives together. Giving away most of what we had (which was not much—remember those bookcases made of three stained boards and cinder blocks?), we packed a very small U-Haul and headed for State College in December of 1969. Three months later Dave was born.

Adjusting to life in the East, we quickly made new friends, enjoyed our comfortable apartment and began to feel very much a part of the small college-town community. I had no reason to believe that this wonderful life I was living would not continue. I found out differently.

My life started changing during the fall of 1974. I was 32 years old.

* * *

I have no specific day to point to, no firm starting date to say, *here is when it all started*. Instead, things began to slowly change. At that time, depression was the furthest thing from my mind. Weren't we all feeling a little out of sorts? After all, it was right after the Vietnam War...when so many young people were questioning values and authority. Many were angry or unhappy. The Kent State shootings during the spring of 1970 and the anger that immediately followed brought disbelief to many of us. The fact that this was happening was horrifying and many of us were incredulous. What was happening to our country? Our values?

By 1973, Gary was settling into his career at Penn State. Our children, now ages three and seven, were enjoying their friends and all that our small rural town had to offer. We loved visiting the sheep barns, traveling to the nearby Amish markets to try the fresh produce and attending the Central Pennsylvania Festival of the Arts every year in July. In State College we could walk most anywhere we wanted to go, feeling safe leaving our doors unlocked while we were gone. The countryside was lush and enchanting.

Wanting to stay at home with Susan and Dave, I chose not to work when they were young. But I remained active and social. Our apartment was right behind six tennis courts so I played tennis with one friend or another most every day while the kids played on an adjacent court. I had wonderful friends whom I saw on a regular basis. We had play dates for our children, shared coffee in the mornings and often met for lunch. During the summer we would pack up lunches and kids and head for the outdoor Olympic-sized pool on campus. Sometimes we would travel to Walnut Acres, an early version of today's health food stores, where we purchased many natural products. I felt fortunate to be able to stay at home with my kids. I basked in the happiness I felt each day and, yes, counted my blessings often.

But over the course of a year, my confidence and joie de vivre slowly began to slip. I started agonizing over decisions that needed to be made, often second-guessing myself after the fact. This was definitely not characteristic of me. The indecision was usually about small things—should I wear the white blouse or the blue one, should I get my hair cut, should I let the kids have a friend over to play? This by itself would have been no cause for alarm, but more bizarre behavior followed. At least, for me it was bizarre. I began to have negative thoughts about my children, comparing them to their peers and regretting what they did not do well, rather than celebrating their strengths as I had always done before.

For example, Susan had always been careful about choosing friends, and I had always felt good about the fact that she was not easily swept into becoming "one of the group." Now, I found myself wishing she was more like her brother, who was outgoing and made friends every chance he got.

But it wasn't only Susan with whom I was disappointed. I obsessed about characteristics of Dave that bothered me...he often befriended kids who misbehaved or were not accepted by others. Rather than seeing this as a good characteristic, that is, reaching out to those who needed friends, I was upset about it. This new side of me was puzzling, but I chose not to dwell on it.

YOU MUST BE MISTAKEN...NOT MY CHILD

But I found it strange that, while I inwardly was disappointed with Susan and Dave, I outwardly became very defensive of them. I didn't want to believe that either one could do anything wrong or have trouble with schoolwork. The reason behind this, I now think, was that I took their misbehaviors and mistakes personally. If they were doing something wrong, it must be I who had caused it. I hadn't raised them right or I wasn't spending enough time with them.

To prevent this negativity from affecting me so severely, my solution (I see now how mistaken I'd been) was to insist they always do the right thing, always make top scores, and always play a great game. If someone let me know that one of them was having trouble with a peer, I *knew* it must have been the other child who had done something wrong rather than *my* child.

This kind of thinking was not at all me. I am a realist. Sure, my kids will screw up. It's part of growing up. Consequences must be imposed so that they can carefully consider choices they make in the future. Because we all learn from our mistakes, not making good choices has a good side. Dave will attest to that; when he was into wrestling for many years, he always maintained that he learned more from his losses than he did from his wins. I believed it was a good way to learn.

CLOUDS ROLL IN

Along with these feelings about my children, I started wishing I led a life that was more exciting. The days were too monotonous. I was itching for *something*. But what? Should I get a graduate degree? Should I visit a friend or relative in another state? A teaching job might be the answer. Wishing for more individuality (ah, those seventies!), I wouldn't always wear my wedding ring so I could be Ann Kochenberger and not just an extension of Gary. You see, in those days women were pretty much a mere appendage of their husbands. When at a cocktail party or someone's home for the evening, people would come up to you and ask, "Who is your husband" or "Do you have any children?"

It was all about being a wife and a mother rather than being just you...an individual who had her own aspirations. That was the way it was and I didn't like it, so I removed the wedding ring, not because I didn't love my husband and children but because I believed that I was much more than a wife and mother.

My head was always full of questions for which I had no answers.

Then, very slowly, over the course of months, the happiness began to erode. The brightness that had surrounded me began to dim. Little by little, first gray, then black clouds covered the sun that had shone down on me all my life. Eventually it would turn to pitch, and all that surrounded me would dramatically change.

CHAPTER 3:
Inner Uncertainty

JOURNAL ENTRY

State College, Pennsylvania November 19, 1974

Have had many urgings to release my thoughts…but no time to do so. It should not be so, but remains a fact. Time seems to dominate. What must life be like for those who allow it to do so completely?

The past few months have left me feeling depressed; dull days filled with rain and clouds seem to adequately reflect all that is in my mind. Life is short, routine if we allow it to be; such routine becomes monotonous and each day becomes much like the previous one.

Change sustains me and makes me feel useful. Underneath all of the uncertainty is the realization that my security is with Gary. I hope he knows how important he is to me yet I know that he often doesn't. He experiences feelings of doubt as far as my love for him is concerned. I'm torn between feigning satisfaction for his security and being honest for my own.

As the sky brightens, so do my spirits. Hopefully, this will continue, but I would detest complete acceptance of my life. Frustrations and desire for something different create, I think, a more completeness of me, a realization of the kind of person I am. At least it provides a beginning…

By the end of that fall, journal entries such as this one were frequently filtering into my writing. As I reread them I saw that my ambivalence was becoming apparent. My mood was fluctuating numerous times over the course of a day or many days, going from sadness and uncertainty to pure happiness. I would reread the journal entries and think another person must have written them. Colors were a big theme in them...first golds and greens, but then grays, blacks...cloudy. It was unsettling to live this way, but I discovered that I was doing so much of the time.

* * *

We had been a part of the State College community for close to five years when my life started to unravel. Ironically, I first noticed these changes in me during my favorite Pennsylvania season...

SNAPSHOT : State College, Pennsylvania Autumn 1974

Autumn is a magical time of year in the East, a season unlike any other. Overnight, it seems, the countryside is transformed. It becomes much more intense, more brilliant with the changes of color.

The hills speak loudly with various hues of gold, brown, orange, yellow and green. The small town and the hills that surround it become like a fairyland.

Maple, oak and sycamore leaves cover lawns and everyone is out raking on the weekends and early evenings. Large leaf piles, pushed out to the street, become jumping places for children, and the air has that smell of dankness and smoke.

On dry days, I never tired of stepping on the leaves to hear their crunching sound. I would see children collecting the most beautiful ones, holding them up to the sun to admire their translucence.

That fall, though, the leaves looked a bit duller. The sky didn't seem as blue.

THE PINPRICKING INCIDENT

One day the principal at the Easterly Parkway Elementary called to tell me that Dave, now a second grader, had been bullying a kindergarten boy every day after school. Apparently he was sticking him with pins.

Of course I couldn't deny it to the principal. After all, everyone already thought I was a bad mother, didn't they? If this were true, this would be verification of it. But inwardly I was sure that there had been a mistake. "Not Dave," I thought. "There is no way that he would pick on a child two years younger."

If he did do this, there must have been a good reason, I thought. My rationalization was this kindergartner must be a bully himself...a hefty boy who was rough and tough. Dave was only defending himself, after all.

I complied with the consequence the school imposed, but deep down I believed that my son had been wronged. Given my new state of mind, I agonized over this for several weeks. The Old Ann would have been disappointed in Dave, but this new person had severe feelings of remorse.

Still certain that Dave was "the victim," I noticed one day that he was walking home from school with a much smaller boy. As the boy walked down the block, I asked Dave who it was. It turned out he was the boy Dave had antagonized...a puny pipsqueak. That was more than a reality check...it was a perfect opportunity to laugh at myself. I must have been feeling more like myself that day because that was exactly what I did.

But then, Susan wanted to be a part of a theater production coming up at the Boal Barn Theater in town. Kids were needed for the cast, so I took her to auditions. We practiced a song and I stressed the importance of smiling and being enthusiastic. She was not selected. Crying on Gary's lap that afternoon, she lamented that she had wanted so badly to be in the production and was sad that she had not been chosen. Me? It was as if I had been stabbed in the heart. If only I had taught her a different song, if only I had put more actions to the song, if only, if only, if only...my mind mulled this disaster over and over again. The fact that Susan was soft spoken, the fact that she was shy and reserved didn't enter into the picture for me. I was the reason she had failed. I was the one who had caused it. Clearly, my thinking was not rational, but I didn't see it that way because I was emotionally incapable of doing so.

METAMORPHOSIS

As the weeks went by, to the outside world my life appeared the same (I was determined it would!), but inwardly I was wracked with uncertainty. I became increasingly introspective, incessantly questioning my ability as wife, mother and friend. Unhappiness, an emotion that I had seldom experienced, was present much of the time.

Why was I so unhappy when I had so much for which to be thankful? Not too long ago I had loved life, but now most of the time I no longer did. I would be happy one day and miserable the next, or I would awaken with feelings of dreading the day only to find myself enjoying it by afternoon or evening.

SEMBLANCE OF NORMALCY

The highs and lows continued through that winter. I immersed myself in my children...their schoolwork and their activities. Keeping busy was a diversion for me, an escape from the clouds that were becoming such a big part of my life. If I were feeling too down, Gary would step in and take over with them. For the most part, though, I continued being their mom as much as I had done so before these shadows began to cover my life.

There were bright spots. The four of us spent much time together. Every Thursday afternoon, we would hold family meetings. This was a time to talk about what we had been doing the past week, to share parts of our lives with one another. It was also an opportunity to discuss any problems, such as completing chores or homework. At the conclusion of these meetings we took turns selecting a family activity for that particular evening. We might go to a movie, have a game night or go to Rec Hall. I still laugh when I think about the bowling days. Gary dreaded the nights when Dave, then age six, got to select the activity because he always picked bowling. Despite pleas and bribes from his father, who disliked bowling intensely, Dave usually stood firm and all of us would get in the car and head for the bowling alley.

SNAPSHOT : State College, Pennsylvania Early spring, 1975

Susan and Dave are off to school. I know I should run if I want to feel better, but I don't want to. I have no energy, no desire to do anything, let alone run. How much longer will this last? It's been over a week of the same...waking to the sinking realization that it is still here. This, in itself, is defeating.

I walk around the house, automatically doing things that need to be done...stacking the dishwasher, making beds, starting laundry. My mind is dull, my body heavy and weighted down. I operate instinctively, knowing that I am in my house and aware of what I am doing. But I feel nothing.

It is terrible to feel nothing. I know that I love my husband and children, but I feel no emotion. It is as if they never were.

I slowly slip into running shorts and shoes, check my watch as I close the front door behind me.

I begin, first walking slowly...down Ellen Avenue, up Nimitz. As I round the corner onto Bradley, I watch as two people steer a wheelchair into a small school van. A severely handicapped child is going to school. She jerks her head up and down, staring ahead with eyes that show no emotion. I count my blessings.

My feet move faster as I get into the run and I am able to let my mind go. These Pennsylvania blocks are much longer than the blocks in Colorado. I always seem to be reminded of this as I run my four-mile course.

My body feels good, lighter and more balanced. My mind is beginning to clear. I continue…down Bradley, up Holman, down Holman, up Nimitz and once I turn back onto Ellen, I slow down the pace until I am back home.

I throw my clothes in the hamper, shower and dress for the day. Only now, four hours after I began my day, do I feel somewhat like my "old self."

Ironically I seem to have more strength during the times I have none. That seems an inconsistent statement, but it isn't. That's how it is.

I can now get things accomplished, so I get busy with errands, housework and dinner as well as make a list of anything else that can be done while I am feeling good.

I am preparing dinner when I look out the back window and see Gary coming through the yard, home from his own four-mile trek from the university.

He sees me and waves. I am happy he is home. It is wonderful to feel so good. I know that this will continue through the evening.

But the next morning…

SNAPSHOT

I know even before I open my eyes. The heavy, sinking feeling in the pit of my stomach tells me. My body feels weighted, and I cannot imagine moving. Thoughts of defeat run through my mind. I know full well the difficulty involved in getting through the day. It takes strength and energy, and I have very little of either.

I continue to lie in bed, motionless, for as long as possible. A heavy weight presses me down. I don't want to get up, but I know that I have to. I think about restructuring the day. What has to be accomplished? What doesn't? Eliminating stress helps, and today it is stressful enough to just get out of bed, but I get up.

It takes tremendous effort to move from the bed to the floor. Each of the small movements that require an arm to pull back the covers, a leg to slide across the sheet and a heel to touch the floor are incredibly difficult. It feels so slow, so heavy. How can I do it again...get through the minute, the next hour, endure the day?

What caused my life to change so drastically defies explanation. For the life of me I could not think of one external reason for this shift. So I looked inside myself for explanation—was it due to my parenting, my marriage, childhood? What?

During the time that my father was in the midst of his residency at Fitzsimmons Hospital, I was born in Denver, Colorado. It was 1942, just before World War II. My father would end up going overseas where he was stationed as part of a medical unit in the Philippines.

My mother and I left Colorado to live with another young mother and her two children while her husband served with my father. We lived in a small house in Carmel, California where, I have always been told, John Steinbeck once peered into my baby buggy where he saw what he called "a very cute baby."

Sometime later, we moved back to Colorado to live with my maternal grandparents on Greenwood Street in my parents' hometown of Pueblo.

I was born into a family of morticians and physicians. My mother's family had been in the mortuary business since her grandfather started T.G. McCarthy Funeral Home at First and Main. I have pictures of my great grandfather atop a white horse, in full beard, leading the parade up Main Street. He was mayor of Pueblo for a term as well as a Colorado State Senator from 1904-06, accomplishments of which the family is quite proud. It was, in fact, during his tenure that Colorado made the decision to recognize Columbus Day as a state holiday.

My great grandparents had seven children who had 20 offspring among them, so my mother and her two brothers grew up with many cousins. They must have taken up several pews each time they attended mass.

I would sometimes ask my grandfather why he had chosen such a morbid line of work and he would respond by telling me that, "Somebody has to do it." I took pride in the fact that he did it well.

My paternal grandfather, W.T.H. Baker, traveled from Illinois to work as a doctor for the Colorado Fuel and Iron Corporation. He eventually went into private practice and then he and two other physicians established the Pueblo Clinic. I think there was a total of 20 to 30 doctors who worked at the clinic. He and four other physicians were the founders of Parkview Episcopal Hospital, where he and, later, my father practiced medicine.

My father, a graduate of Colorado College, went on to earn his medical degree from Northwestern University in Chicago. Both Dr. Bakers were highly respected in their professions. My mother told us stories about when she and my father lived in Evanston, Illinois while he attended medical school. They had very little money, but would save their pennies so that they could watch the Cubs play baseball at Wrigley Field. It cost 20 cents each for a ticket, so they didn't go as often as they would have liked. She said that they had holiday dinners with other young couples in their apartment building, and I remember her describing one Thanksgiving when she and another wife were removing a large turkey from the oven, ready to place it on the platter. The turkey fell and skidded across the kitchen floor. They looked at one another, picked the turkey up, put it on the platter and served it to the guests. This was during the Depression.

My sister Susan, a year and a half younger, and I would accompany our father to the clinic on Sunday afternoons while he "wrote histories" of the patients whom he had seen that week. I well remember the fiasco that occurred one afternoon. Susan and I were in the records room where there was a large ladder on wheels that reached close to the ceiling. This ladder enabled those who worked in records to retrieve the files of patients that were on the top shelves. This was, of course, long before the days of computers, so everything was documented on paper.

We were taking turns pushing one another quite fast because we never did anything halfway. When the ladder would hit the end of the row, it would abruptly stop because it was supposed to. Well, she was on top and not holding on tightly enough. She flew off and landed on a glass-top desk with a thud. My father took her home in a cast from the knee down that night. Susan and I were adventurous, to say the least, but it always seemed to be she who got injured... stitches and broken bones.

I was very close to my father, and have always had tremendous admiration for him, certainly as a physician, but far more so because of the way he lived his life. My father was probably the most tolerant person I have ever known. He judged people on the basis of their kindness, their work ethic and their ability to help others, never on social standing or how much education they had. He was able to see beyond outward appearances into the very hearts of others. He was always smiling and joking; he was a man of great integrity, and I truly believe this is what attracted me to Gary. He has many of my father's qualities.

I would often accompany my father on "house calls"—remember them? I would sit in the car, listening to *The Wayward Wind, Cross Over the Bridge* and other tunes popular back in the mid-fifties. I loved being with him, and always jumped at the chance to go.

He allowed me to watch when he sewed up people who had been hurt, or when he performed gall bladder operations or appendectomies and delivered babies. I would don hospital scrubs and mask, and stand in the background. I remember that there was a glassed-in room from which I was able to see babies make their way into the world. I once saw twins delivered, a surprise to all in the delivery room.

The nurses loved Dr. Baker and most were supportive of me tagging along. A few were not, but it never seemed to bother my father. I guess he thought that he had special privileges, and in a way he did, since my grandfather had been the one to establish the hospital. I never remember seeing any other children with their doctor fathers (there were no women doctors back then that I ever knew.)

During the fifties the most important thing a father could do for his children was to provide for them. Mothers ran the households while fathers worked all day. Very few fathers spent time doing things exclusively *with* their children, but this was not considered a negative. That was the way it was supposed to be.

My brother and sisters and I were fortunate, though, because our father spent quite a bit of time with us once he arrived home. I would sit on the steps of the front porch with my ball glove on my lap, waiting for his car to drive up. He would toss fly balls and grounders to me until he tired of running after any errant throws I would make. This was a daily ritual.

Once my sister Susan and I were old enough, we organized a softball team comprised of junior high friends. Our dad loved to watch us practice and play and would drive us to out of town games. We were city champs twice, after which we went to the state tournament in Denver where we came home with the winners' trophy one of those years. It was great fun.

Aside from the many softball games that we played during those tournament weekends, my father took the opportunity to make this a learning experience as well. As a team, we had approached merchants for donations that could be used for lodging and food while in Denver. In order to save on motel cost, the entire team was able to stay at my Aunt Betty and Uncle Lynn's big house on Detroit Street. There were six bedrooms, plenty of room for the team, my father and Mr. Zupanzic, the father of our pitcher. Barbara Zupanzic was one phenomenal pitcher, and it was due to her and our incredible catcher, Donna Davis, that the team was able to excel.

The monies saved on motel moved over to the general fund, and, because of this surplus, we now had enough for entertainment. We spent one evening at Elich's, a Denver amusement park and, before we left the ball field, each girl was given a specific amount of money to be used for both food and entertainment that night.

My father died of a massive heart attack when he was only forty-eight. At the time, I didn't think that was young, but I now know differently. His death was a tremendous loss, not only to his family, but also to the community. Even today, people tell stories of admiration about him, his generosity and his kindness. I was the oldest of the siblings; my mother had five more to raise, and the youngest was only five. It was very difficult, not financially, because we were well provided for, but emotionally. So difficult, in fact, that my mother became an alcoholic, and my younger brothers and sister were raised entirely differently than were Susan and I.

It would have been far more difficult had God not sent an angel to us when my brother, Bill, was six weeks old. My mother hired someone to help with all that had to be done around the house, which included taking care of Susan, Bill and me.

Jennie Perez walked into our lives one morning, and never left. She was an amazing person...kind, patient and loving. Soft-spoken and always happy, Jennie walked with a profound limp that was the result of a broken leg when she was brought into the world. That limp was Jennie's sole flaw, if you think of a limp as a flaw. Years later my father told her that he would see to it that she had it repaired and he would incur the cost, but she declined his offer.

My brothers and sisters were particularly fortunate that Jennie was so much a part of our family by the time my father died. It was she who provided much needed stability at a time when our lives had been so painfully disrupted. Recently married, I no longer lived at home, but it gave me great comfort knowing that Jennie was always at the house.

SISTERS AND BROTHERS

I have always been extremely close to my sister Susan. Given that we are just seventeen months apart in age, I guess this is not surprising. Susan is not like me in many ways and, it is for this reason, I think, that we have never really been competitive like so many sisters are.

Susan is reserved and shy while I am outgoing and verbal. She is pragmatic while I have a tendency to be spontaneous. I am the risk taker, something that often got me in trouble while growing up. Susan had tons of friends; I certainly didn't lack friendships, but everyone loves Susan. I was the student. She was the athlete... the reason for sprained and broken ankles and hernia operations. We both played softball, but she had natural athletic ability backed by a fierce competitiveness.

I remember that she helped me practice when she convinced me to try out for cheerleader at the end of my junior year in high school. She had been on the squad for her sophomore year and was trying out again. We practiced constantly in front of the large picture window on our side porch, a great place to watch our reflections. On the day of the tryouts, after four of the slots had been selected, it was announced that, since there was a tie for the fifth spot, two girls would have to do their routine again. Susan was one of the two, and she was called first. Afterwards, while the other girl was trying out, Susan held onto me, saying that she just knew she wouldn't make it. I knew she would because if she had not been chosen fifth, I would have declined my spot, which would have allowed her to move from sixth to fifth. After all, she was my mentor here, and I would never have been able to enjoy my time as a cheerleader knowing that I was the reason she would not be among the rest of us. That's what sisters do for one another.

When the names of the new cheerleaders were announced, Susan was one of those selected. I didn't have to step down after all, and we had a wonderful year together cheering for the Central Wildcats.

Once I was married, I missed her terribly. It had always been the two of us...sharing the same room, playing on teams together, sharing many of the same friends and talking late into the night. We also shared secrets—and we helped one another. But it was at sharing clothes where I drew the line. Susan was very careless about organization as far as her bedroom went. What she wore on Monday would be on the bottom of a pile on her bedroom chair, outfits from the rest of the week piled atop. It drove me crazy, particularly when she wanted to wear something of mine. My clothes were organized by color, from light to dark hues within each. I never wanted to share because I knew she wouldn't take care of it, and because I might not be able to find it after she used it. I would often see her walking in the school halls, wearing an article of clothing that she had grabbed from my closet after I left for school. I would run after her, yelling at her all the way down to the classroom. One year we had Latin 1 together, and poor Mr. Lloyd found himself serving as referee a number of times because Susan would walk into class wearing one of my sweaters.

I have always maintained that I am really not the oldest child because I have a cousin, Bill Kemper, who is really like a brother to all of us. His mother, my Aunt Betty was my father's sole sibling. My cousin, who was named for my father, had much admiration for him. He would come down from Denver to spend weekends at our house, particularly following the death of his father. We would travel to Denver many times a year, so we saw Aunt Betty, Uncle Lynn and Bill often. Once Bill was married, he and his wife Carol, and later the three sons they would have, spent holidays with all of us.

Because of the fact that Susan and I were born right before and during the time my father served in World War II, there is a large gap between the two of us and our four younger siblings. Bill arrived when we were six and five, Ray two years later, followed by Betsy two and a half years later and, lastly, by Bob who was born two years after Betsy. We found Bill pesky, Ray sweet, Betsy cute as a button and Bob lots of fun while we were growing up. Today the six of us are very close.

I loved growing up in Pueblo, as do most others from my hometown. People who live there have a sort of camaraderie, a bond that immediately becomes apparent once you learn that they, too, are from there. When we were in college in Boulder, people would make fun of Pueblo and looked down on it as being "beneath" other cities because of the steel mill. Some even referred to it as Phew Town. We merely winked at one another, confident that we knew differently.

I think I loved the diversity of Pueblo the most. It has a large percentage of Mexican Americans, so I got a good look into their rich culture and, if lucky, the opportunity to taste the food that they made so well. There were areas in town in which Italians lived too. And, nearby lived the "Bo johns," people from eastern European countries like Poland and Slovakia We have never known anyone from elsewhere who has heard the term Bo johns, so we like to think that it's a unique Pueblo term.

When we were young, we played with the neighborhood kids...softball games in the street, kick the can at night. We sledded down Van Buren "hill," which we thought was steep but isn't. We made Christmas tree forts in a hole on a vacant lot a block from our house. We would have snowball fights and, if we were lucky, our fathers would pull us around snow-packed streets on sleds, whipping us around as we turned corners. Afterward, we would make cups of hot chocolate for all.

Keating Junior High and Central High School, across the street, were about five blocks from my house. We walked every day, just as we had walked the seven blocks to Carlile Elementary School. I doubt if car-pooling was part of anybody's vocabulary at that time. Because of this, along with the fact that we didn't get television until I was in seventh grade, we got lots of exercise and were nice and trim.

* * *

For a while I had convinced myself that these extreme mood changes were simply due to my philosophical nature and that my reflections were the result, but I soon had to admit that it was much more than being theoretical. I finally decided that it must be due to a restlessness within that would eventually dissipate. I waited...and waited...and waited...

SNAPSHOT : State College, Pennsylvania April, 1975

I sit in the dark on the couch in the small den. Feelings of regret and emptiness dominate my thoughts. It's too difficult to pretend that I am the person I used to be. I'm tired of trying to disguise my inadequacies.

Conversation and laughter drift up from downstairs. Not so very long ago I had been laughing too, talking about children, travels and catching up on everyone's news.

I know all those people to whom the conversation and laughter belong.

They are my friends, people on whom I can depend, but I don't want to be with them. So I sit alone in the darkness.

CHAPTER 4:
Black Storm Clouds Threaten

JOURNAL ENTRY
State College, Pennsylvania May 16, 1975

Feelings of disorientation and paranoia have become dominant in my life. The world seems to be closing in, and I am spinning and uneven. Always aware of each movement, sometimes just part of a movement, creates a strange feeling.

I am afraid I will lose control of words and responses, talking gibberish at any moment. I am often "outside myself looking in."

By spring that year, sleep had been replaced by insomnia and happiness had been replaced by sadness. My confidence was gone. I had constant worries about my self-worth. I found that sometimes I couldn't complete an intelligent sentence. I became paranoid (my friends hate me), and had difficulty completing mundane tasks such as grocery shopping, going to the bank or getting gas for the car. I lacked the concentration necessary to read the newspaper or even watch television. I would sit, staring into space, wondering what was happening to me.

It seemed as if the world I had known had been transformed. I had been abducted and taken away, to an inner world filled with despair, hopelessness and fear. Where had the old Ann gone?

OUTWARD DECEPTION

I became a master of deception. To the outside world, I was the energetic, happy person I had always been (and my friends were shocked when they discovered much later that this had been far from the case). Pity is something I have never wanted, nor do I want others to dwell on my health, so my dark secret was shared only with Gary. I made him *promise* that he wouldn't tell anyone that something was wrong.

He kept that promise. Each time he encouraged me to talk with my sister or a friend, I knew that I simply couldn't. It would have made me appear weak in their eyes. I wanted to keep the identity I had to those who lived on the outside. The inside was in chaos and I couldn't have coped with the questions, shock or looks of sympathy from others. I didn't want to hear "Poor Ann," or "Is there anything I can do to help?" How could any of them even begin to understand all with which I had to contend when I didn't understand it myself?

More importantly, I never let Dave and Susan know. To them, I was always just Mom.

* * *

As days and weeks went by, this darkness, this feeling of being out of focus, would periodically be replaced by light, and then the darkness would once again surround me. I never knew when my world would change. This thing, this depression (I didn't yet know what it was) would remain for a week or two, and then I would wake one morning knowing that "the old Ann" had returned.

Just like that, I would bask in the awareness of this, loving my life once again, interacting with friends, doing things with the kids, and running on high speed because I was coming to learn that it wouldn't last. And, as predicted, the depression would return and I would become an entirely different person. Once again, no one realized this because I would not let them, but *I* knew and it was beginning to be terrifying.

Severe depression is a petrifying illness over which one has no control. It can disappear overnight, in seconds, or it can slowly dissipate over days. Knowing this only increases anxiety and causes one to hesitate before making plans or committing to anything. It meant that I remained home, alone in the world of despair that surrounded me. It was a struggle just dealing with the unpredictability of my inner world, so I closed myself off from the outside world.

LIFE LOSES FOCUS

Being out of focus aptly describes the onset of these symptoms. No longer could I see things clearly. Looking at all that I had in my life was unsatisfying now. What was happening to me? How can it be that everything had been so wonderful just a short time ago and now I can find no joy in anything? It made no sense. My *life* was making no sense.

My mind was beginning to work overtime as I tried to analyze each puzzling situation, *knowing* full well that I was not looking at things clearly. But knowing that something is not true and *feeling* as if it is not are two different things, and, as I found out much later, those who experience the beginning of a depressive episode view everything with negativity.

The best way to describe it is that reality blurred. The focus of a camera is out of whack, as if I were a crazed photographer who kept adjusting the lens, frantically attempting to bring my life back into focus, but not able to. I made no sense, had no confidence to even leave the house. I grew more and more paranoid, to the point I was suspicious of *everyone's* motives. My anxiety was so acute that I felt strangled. And so I lay on the couch or sat staring into space, unable to cope.

SNAPSHOT State College, Pennsylvania Spring 1975

And there I remained, a prisoner within the abyss into which I had fallen, convinced that I was useless to everyone around me. I was an albatross that was choking the joy out of others. I started thinking about suicide. It seemed to be the only way out. I thought about it often, and, in a bizarre way, the idea provided comfort. It was, after all, the only thing over which I did have control and would be a way to end the mental and physical pain.

CHAPTER 5:
Depressed? Not me.

I feel like a spiral...spinning...spinning...spinning, going nowhere except in a continuous circle. Is life merely one continuous circle, repetitious of things that differ only slightly as we grow older? My mind wanders and makes me continually question what is of value.

Demands, many trivial, fill my time.

Solitude is what I seek, yet am not allowed to obtain. <u>I seek to be alone within myself rather than allow myself to be known.</u> The secrecy within all of us makes us unique, and that mystique is what makes others want to know more.

If our thoughts were exposed, the shadows that conceal our identity would be erased and, with it, the desire to further know.

My symptoms had now been growing progressively worse. I went from somewhat depressed that past fall to *Oh my God, what is the matter with me?* by spring. My journal captured my fears well. No words can adequately describe the complexity of depression, but the underlined sentence from my journal entry is revealing of how I presented myself to others. I was "Ann" to acquaintances and "Mrs. Kochenberger" to my students, but nameless to myself.

MY THREE IDENTITIES

This ability to act differently when around others in order to disguise my despair is called dissociation. When one dissociates from something, she/he becomes detached and that is exactly what I did. I didn't realize that there was a term for what I was doing. I just knew that I needed to revert to the person I had been when I was well because that was the person everyone knew. It was a conscious choice and, fully aware of what I was doing, it worked much of the time. But, if I was too severely depressed, I was not able to pull the role-playing off. I would have to remain as I really was, canceling appointments and/or social engagements because I knew that I simply could not function around others.

When I think about it further, there were three parts of me rather than two. One was the Ann I pretended to be, the second was the depressed person I was while the third was the healthy me who was neither sick nor acting. When depression was present, however, the third person was nowhere near; the other two people changed places as situations presented themselves. Confusing? It's confusing just to try to explain how confusing it was within my mind.

It could have been far worse. Had I been *unaware* of these other sides of me being able to "come out" and pretend that all was well, I would have had a more serious psychiatric disorder known as dissociative identity disorder (DID) also known as multiple personality disorder.

Just nine months after I had started feeling badly, I was so out of control that I was close to not being able to function at all. My days were a series of endless obligations that I desperately struggled to fulfill. I felt like I was just going through the motions. I was trapped on a merry-go-round of monotony with no brass ring to grab. Happiness was an emotion of long ago. I had forgotten what it felt like. Other feelings eluded me. I felt no anger, had no curiosity for anything. I was just robotically going through the motions.

It is frightening to always be "inside your mind" and not be able to think beyond it. The months crept by.

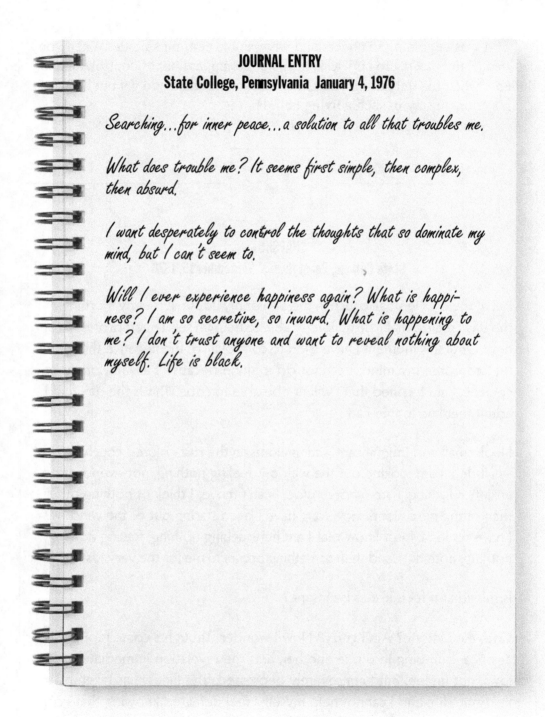

JOURNAL ENTRY
State College, Pennsylvania January 4, 1976

Searching...for inner peace...a solution to all that troubles me.

What does trouble me? It seems first simple, then complex, then absurd.

I want desperately to control the thoughts that so dominate my mind, but I can't seem to.

Will I ever experience happiness again? What is happiness? I am so secretive, so inward. What is happening to me? I don't trust anyone and want to reveal nothing about myself. Life is black.

And then, the present ceased to exist. One day it simply vanished. *All* of my time was focused on regretting the past and worrying about the future. I ruminated constantly...*every* waking moment. It was exhausting!

I was beginning to understand why people commit suicide. When you can't eat, can't sleep, are hopeless, have no feeling, are out of control, anxiety ridden...when the only thing you *can* control is the chance to get out of all of it...it's crazy to stay in such a living hell. Isn't it?

Wait! I *was* crazy...suicide? Me?

SNAPSHOT
State College, Pennsylvania September 15, 1976

I sit alone on the small couch in the den of my house. It is early morning of the day I realize that I am no longer able to help myself. I need professional help. Until this moment I have tried to control all of the negative thoughts that consume my mind. I cannot do it alone because I am no longer in control. I am terrified that I will not be able to cope. This is the day that I admit that I no longer can.

I look small and insignificant, sitting alone on the rust-colored couch in the small den. I am looking out the window, feeling nothing, not even fear or anxiety. Nothing. I am empty inside. I can't move; I think of nothing other than sitting here alone. How long have I been staring out of the window? I have no idea. I just know that I am here, seeing nothing, feeling nothing, nothing, nothing...and then something occurs to me for the very first time.

Is this what it feels like to be insane?

God, am I insane? Am I crazy? Now I wonder. Thoughts come rapidly, all at once, bumping into one another, and the revelation immediately follows: not insane. But I am severely depressed. This illness has taken over my entire life and I cannot help myself. I feel defeated knowing that I am incapable of erasing any of these thoughts.

And now I realize that I have allowed this to go on much too long.

HELP

But *why* had I waited so long? I have always respected the medical and psychiatric professions and have always taken comfort in the belief that I would not hesitate to take advantage of them, and yet, here I was. It had been two long years since depression began to filter into my life, and only now was it occurring to me that I needed a doctor's help.

I continued to sit there that day, thinking through all that had just become so apparent. I slowly began to grasp my failure to recognize the obvious. I had assumed that a person who suffered a nervous breakdown was insane. I was not insane! But I knew I was not normal either. I also knew—finally—that I needed help.

I found this incredulous that it had not occurred to me before *now*. What should have been perfectly clear wasn't obvious at all: I wasn't insane, but I was mentally ill.

I went to the phone that morning to make an appointment with Dr. Paul Carney, our family physician. Dr. Carney was respected for his expertise as well as for his genuine concern for his patients. My admiration for him grew immediately because he recognized that I needed a mental health specialist. He referred me to a psychologists' group in town, and when I left his office with a prescription for an antidepressant in my hand and a number in my pocket, I naively thought that this was all that was needed and that my mental problems would soon be gone.

I went right home, dialed a number I would soon know by heart and made an appointment the following week with Dr. David A. (Sandy) Macdonald. I felt a sense of relief and, if I am remembering correctly, a slight smile forced my lips upward for the first time in many, many months.

CHAPTER 6:
A Change of Direction

SNAPSHOT
State College, Pennsylvania September 28, 1976

The building is old and narrow. It faces the main street of the small town in which I have lived for the past six years. I know where it is because I have passed it many times on my way to other places.

It stands at the corner of South Burroughs and College Avenue. Sitting directly across from the campus of Penn State University, it was someone's home long ago.

But, like so many houses in the East, it was purchased for business purposes and converted into offices. It looks like some of the other houses that line the block.

I ignore the other houses, but not this one. This one is different.

On this September morning I carefully choose what I will wear. I am most comfortable in casual clothes, so I am wearing one of my favorite outfits… an olive green, soft pair of pants with matching jacket and a long-sleeved silky print shirt. It is definitely me…informal, unpretentious. As I put it on, the familiarity feels safe and secure. Each leg easily slips into the softness of the material; I tuck in the smooth shirt and effortlessly slide the zipper of the slacks up, securing the closure with a final snap. My small frame is thin and smooth, my weight is several pounds over one hundred, easy to maintain running after two small children and lacking sleep and nutrition.

I slide into soft tan leather hiking shoes with leather laces. My hair is straight and shoulder length, parted in the middle. I feel satisfied as I catch my reflection in the hall mirror before closing the front door behind me.

It is autumn in the East, its most beautiful season. I walk briskly, each step concealing the huge, dry leaves that cover the sidewalk.

As I open the small door of the building that is old and narrow, steep, constricted stairs lead high up to the second floor beyond. Nothing else is visible. That's all there is…steep, narrow stairs climbing straight up.

I stand there for a moment, pausing before I begin the ascent. All the reasons that have brought me to this place seem simultaneously stuck in my mind. What strange paths we travel as we weave in and out of each day, so many of them unpredictable.

When did the unpredictability begin? I can't remember now. I know that it occurred slowly, over time, until it became a part of my consciousness. And then, one day two years ago, some of my thoughts moved from my mind onto paper.

Walking slowly up the narrow stairs to the second floor, I hear my footsteps touch each step. The top is stark, old and dark. It smells of musty air that has been there a long time. I see the door: David A. Macdonald, PhD

My hand closes around the knob as I twist it slowly but firmly. I open the door. Feeling anxious, I step inside; full of anticipation and curiosity, I am confident today. I step into the room and look around.

A soft couch sits in the small room. Beside it, an easy chair with wide arms, a small braided rug. A modest table rests beside the couch. The room is neat and casual, uncluttered. It is clean and clear and quiet, very quiet. I sit on the edge of the couch and wait for someone to come.

It is very still in the room. Carefully tended plants are scattered through-out. Sun streams in through the clear glass, sunrays dance in the light. I can hear myself breathing in and out, in and out, slowly and softly. I am comfortable in this room that emits feelings of welcome, calm, softness and tranquility.

Sensing a slight movement in the doorway, I look up. Standing there is a man who appears to be in his late thirties, of delicate build, dark hair and slight features. He is wearing casual shoes, slacks and a sweater. His eyes are a deep blue, his demeanor calm and caring, reassuring. He smiles as he extends his hand.

"Hi, I'm Sandy Macdonald," he says.

"I don't know where to begin," I begin. And then all the confusion, the frustration, the wanting to live but hoping to die comes tumbling out all at once. The days and months of despair deep within my thinking move slowly forward.

And so begins a professional relationship that in a sense becomes a friend-ship that extends over the next ten years.

I had been nervous all weekend before that first appointment. But I also was experiencing something I had not experienced in a very long time—hope. I abruptly changed directions that day because I had taken a step toward recovery. I had finally reached out to someone else because I felt that I had no other options. I could no longer deal with all of this on my own.

Thinking that I was mentally ill and reaching outside myself to address it were two entirely different things. My admission that I could no longer cope, I came to see, was a turning point in my life that would eventually lead to my feeling better...but that road would prove to be a very long one. No quick fix, no magic pill. The journey would be neither direct nor smooth. Many roadblocks would prove deterrents, and forks in the road would result in having to make choices that would, inevitably, make this journey a very difficult one, not only for me but for my family as well.

THERAPY AT LAST

"Doctor" did not fit Dr. Macdonald at all. This man was way too casual, too friendly. He wasn't stern or aloof at all. I was immediately relieved and knew that I had made the right choice. He had introduced himself as Sandy, so that was what I called him from that day on.

He had an easy, tranquil manner and a smile that emitted understanding, caring and respect. He would ask about my journal writing. Was I writing every day? What was I writing? How was I feeling? Was it getting easier to cope? Was I tolerating the medication well?

"Tell me an example of a time when you feel lack of confidence," he would ask. "Do you feel that way at home sometimes?"

I would tell him about situations where feelings of inferiority had come up, or times when I would have difficulty concentrating or talking intelligently. All this time, Sandy sat there patiently, smiling slightly, taking notes and making me feel comfortable.

At the end of that first session, I scheduled another, something I would continue to do off and on for years. I quickly discovered that this was one of the few places where I could be myself and I looked forward to each appointment.

* * *

I didn't tell Gary until after a couple of sessions. His initial reaction was hurt, then concern.

"Why did you keep this from me?" he asked. "Don't we always share things? Why didn't you tell me how dreadful it has been for you?"

I knew that he felt shut out, but how could I tell him what was happening to me when I didn't know myself? I had to have something specific to tell, some indication I was taking positive steps. I have never regretted my decision to delay discussing all of it with him. I knew that he would feel better knowing that I had at least some sense of direction. I asked him to attend my next session with Sandy.

During the sessions that followed, Gary listened intently as I spoke about the panic I was feeling...how I had lost the life I once had...how I had become an entirely different person, a person who was mysterious, unpredictable and completing lacking in confidence. He soon realized that I was petrified.

Afterwards, riding home in the car, there was no conversation at first. We were both subdued in our thinking. I was thinking I was severely ill and recovery would be long and difficult. I believe he thought that too. We had much work ahead of us...reading, discussing, communicating.

"I thought Sandy was great," he said finally. "I felt completely at ease with him." I agreed. It was easy to be yourself with Sandy because it felt like having a serious conversation with a friend...á friend who happened to be a professional in an area that I desperately needed to know more about.

From that time on, Gary and I talked freely, sparing no feelings. We both knew that we had to be completely honest before I could begin to get well; this was something Sandy had stressed. We purchased two copies of every book recommended, simultaneously reading and discussing them before we returned for the next session. I was grateful and very touched by my husband's commitment to my recovery. Not many spouses would be this deeply concerned (this is a colossal understatement). Once again, I counted my blessings, knowing how fortunate I was to have such an incredible husband. I was not going to have to take the long journey alone. He would be with me every step of the way.

I don't know how many times I walked up those narrow steps to that small, uncluttered room and sat upon Sandy's soft couch, but the literal and figurative steps I had taken the first day in therapy were the beginning of my salvation. I didn't know then how difficult the years ahead would be or how many years there would be, but it felt good to get started.

CHAPTER 7:
A Lifetime of Loving

Over the years to follow, Gary became my confidant extraordinaire. He always was there for me and had such good advice. Giving good advice was nothing new for him, though. Even before we were married, he provided a balanced view of the world, and many of our friends have confided in him over the years. His advice is given in a way that is never judgmental, and people appreciate the comfort his conversations provide. As far back as I can remember (which is *really* far) classmates have been drawn to his fairness, his kindness and his acceptance…

Gary always tells people that we met in kindergarten, but Gary tends to exaggerate. The truth is that we didn't meet until we were in the first grade. We had Miss Albertson, a teacher who had taught my dad when he was that age. She really was wonderful. I remember that we all respected her, but no one feared her (instilling fear was "in" back then). As was typical in those days, desks were arranged in long rows and I remember Miss Albertson passing out our supplies…the boxes of crayons, their scent I can still remember if I close my eyes and picture the scene.

I don't remember Gary in particular until third grade, though. That was the year I first had a boy friend, and it was Gary. That next year and the two that followed, he gave me a Christmas gift. I remember them well…Santa figures that were candles, a green plastic purse, and a necklace, the silver beads of which resembled small BB's that are used in BB guns. Each year, after he silently handed me my gift on the playground after school, he would run away.

When we were in sixth grade, about twenty of us from the class took ballroom dancing, something our parents thought we needed to do since we would be going into seventh grade the following year. A rite of passage. Interestingly, Gary's mother, my future mother-in-law taught the class. It was a natural choice because she was a dancer and, at one time, had her own dancing school. We enjoyed learning the dances, but also saw those Wednesday evenings as a way to spend time with our friends. One day, I got a note in school, handed to me by "you know whom." The note was short and to the point.

Dear Ann,
Wednesday night at dancing class, Wally is going to kiss Nancy and I am
going to kiss you.
Love,
Gary

Oh, how I wish I had saved that note. I would have been able to use it as material for bribing to get what I wanted through the years. (Of course, I didn't need the note to get what I wanted, but it would have been fun to have it). But I digress. I couldn't tell Nancy fast enough and we anxiously awaited our first kiss.

At the end of the evening, the four of us went to the back of the Lattimer house where we experienced our first "romantic" kiss. I must say that it was anything but romantic. Robotic is a much more apt description. There was no movement of lips or neck, no arms around me...not at all like the movies, but then I guess when you have never practiced, you do the best you can. To this day, when I tell this story, people are astonished to learn that a third grade "love note" and the sixth grade "kiss" were from Gary.

He has always been in the picture and, relatively speaking, it was much easier for him to be there the first twenty-eight years of our lives together. More astonishing is that he has been there for the subsequent ones. But then, he is one astonishing man.

* * *

Both of my parents thought that Gary was wonderful, right from the start...even though I didn't. I think my dad liked him because he played sports and he had a crew cut, two qualities that were strong indications that someone was "really cool" in my dad's eyes. My mom loved him because he was so polite, but also because she knew his mother from PTA and the fact that they both often served as Room Mothers. You know, the mothers who call other mothers and have them provide cupcakes, cookies and punch for class parties.

The Kochenbergers are great people. They are kind and considerate, always have smiles on their faces and are willing to share with others. Gary's mother, who would later be my mother-in-law, had many children so my mother could relate to her in that respect as well. It always seemed to be those mothers who were busiest who also did the most at the school.

I remember being at a junior high school football game on a freezing cold fall night. I saw Gary's dad sitting up in the bleachers with a wool blanket on his lap.

"Get under this blanket, gal," he urged. "It's cold out there."

It was and I did, thanking him for sharing such a commodity on such a cold night.

And what I remember most about Gary in grade school is how kind he was to others. A class leader, he included everyone in games, looked out for the underdogs and always had a huge smile on his face. Dimples deepened his cheeks and he often wore a white tee shirt, the bottom of which exposed his stomach. He would fight for his friends at recess if necessary and I guess it was necessary. His mother has told us that she received a 'Gary's fighting again' call from our principal, Mr. Lyle, every day. I think she exaggerates because I neither remember daily fights nor Gary frequently being called out of class.

* * *

Gary and I dated in our sophomore year, but not exclusively. He would ask me out when he would come to the house, always asking in front of my mother, who would say, "Oh, how nice. I'm sure she would love to go, wouldn't you, Ann?" I would mutter under my breath because I really wouldn't "love to go," but found myself going nevertheless.

We broke up at the end of our sophomore year and dated others during our junior year. I was really into studying, choir, junior play, and student government and, of course, friends, so I only casually dated now and then.

At the end of that year, I took the train to California to stay with my Uncle Tim for a while. It was while I was away that I guess I did a lot of thinking and one of the things that I gave a lot of thought to was how great a guy Gary was. He *had* been my first boy friend, and I distinctly remember falling in love with him one night when we were at a dance our sophomore year. Like young people do, though, I had fallen out of love by the next year, but I remembered how good it had felt and wanted to be in that place again. So, I called his house the afternoon I returned home from California.

I told him what I had been thinking and asked if I could see him. I did...we talked and decided to "get back together." I felt great about the Gary part, but I felt badly about the fact that I had to give back a class ring to the boy with whom I was going steady because I knew how upset he would be.

GARY: "Ann and I grew up a few blocks from each other, went to school together, and were boy friend/girl friend on and off throughout the years. She was attractive, smart, popular, athletic, and generally everything a boy might be looking for in a girl to date. I guess it is fair to say that to varying degrees, I had a crush on Ann from 1st grade all the way into high school.

"The feelings one has for another—particularly amorous feelings—are probably best represented by a continuum rather than a dichotomy. Who can say with certainty when a youthful crush transitions from crush to love?

"All I know is that I remember vividly, as if it were just yesterday, the day I fell in love with Ann. It hit me like a ton of bricks and put in motion a lifetime of loving. Of course I didn't know at the time what the outcome would be. I only knew that something profound had happened.

"The day in question came in the fall of 1958. I visited Ann at her house as I had done many times before. One of her siblings answered the door and showed me into the living room where I took a seat as they went to fetch Ann. A few minutes later she came to greet me wearing a black-and-brown checkered dress with a full skirt. She was in a happy mood and twirled around as if dancing as she entered the room. As she approached, I was struck by the realization of just how beautiful she was to me. It was a special, almost magical moment—one that I'd not experienced before or after. I was just a sixteen-year-old kid but I nonetheless knew at that moment that I was in love. We had talked about love, but all of a sudden the notion of love inexplicably and unexpectedly took on a captivating new and deeper meaning.

"To this day I'm not sure why things happened the way they did that day in 1958. I've never had any doubt, however, that that was the day my feelings for Ann transitioned from crush to something far more substantial and important. That was the day I fell 'madly in love' with her."

* * *

We were married right out of high school and were both eighteen years old. Most people back then were married by age twenty-one. If you weren't married by age 24, it was looking doubtful that you would ever marry! We chose to have Susan when we were that age because we felt we were "getting up there" in age. Women had far fewer options in those days. If they worked, they either did day care, were teachers or nurses. No one traveled before college. You went to college right after high school, got a job and stayed with it. In Pueblo, many who did not go to college went to work at the mill.

We lived in Boulder for eight years, during which time I received my BS degree with a double major in history and elementary education. In addition, I took graduate classes (in history) while teaching and raising Susan.

Gary completed his BS in electrical engineering, and began the interview process. He interviewed with Texas Instruments, 3M and several other companies, and received offers from a few. Upon returning from yet another interview, he told me that he didn't want to enter industry just yet. Rather, he would like to work on an MBA degree. I was astounded because he had said nothing about this route, but I was certainly supportive.

Before he was well into the MBA, he had decided to continue and pursue a PhD that he earned at the end of the 1969 fall semester. His grandfather Kochenberger never could understand why he kept going to school.

"Why don't you just get a nice job, Sonny Boy?" he would repeatedly inquire.

Gary would explain his desire for further education, and Grandpa Koch would say that he understood, which was probably not true. But I know that his grandparents were proud of him.

BOULDER DAYS

We lived in three different styles of apartments during our years as college students. First we had a buffet that consisted of a room with a galley kitchen off to the side, a built-in desk, a couch and a chair. The couch unfolded into a bed, which we would remake into a couch each morning. The kitchen table was flat against the wall when not in use, pulled up and locked in place when it was. The tiny bathroom had a closet outside, and this was the only storage we had other than the dresser that sat in the living room. Hey, it was just fine for our needs, but it did mean a lot of togetherness.

The following year we moved into a one-bedroom and felt as if we had oceans of room. The bedroom was just a bedroom. Wow! We were there for several years, until we moved into a two-bedroom three months prior to the arrival of Susan.

We had many neighbors and enjoyed them all. The Moores lived nearby and their front door was only a few steps from ours. Margaret was Canadian and Larry was a doctoral student in management in the College of Business. He and Gary would have great conversations and we all had interesting discussions, mostly about life. We had great respect for the way the Moores looked at the world, the way they respected their children and the way they always reached out to others. We are fortunate that they came into our lives and remain friends with them to this day.

They almost didn't get into our lives, if truth were told. We would always stop and talk with their youngster, David, in his playpen and, often, Margaret would be sitting on the back steps. One day, when I was passing by alone, she suggested to me that Gary and I might like to come over one evening.

I was pleased about this prospect, but when I told Gary, he was rather distressed.

"Why, what could we possibly have in common with the two of them? They are much older than we are!"

They *were* much older...eight and nine years older...but we have always laughed about that, particularly since it turned out that we had much in common. And, we learned a valuable lesson: never say never because you may be giving up something golden.

Among all our friends in Boulder, I always seemed to be the one to arrange social gatherings. No one has ever let me forget the night eight of us attended a university production of *Oedipus Rex*. Convinced that we needed more culture in our lives, I bought all the tickets and we set off for the auditorium one Saturday night, only to discover we were attending a rather unusual rendition of this Shakespeare play. It was presented in the Japanese Nu (pronounced "no") tradition in which lines are said with no emotion, monotonically spoken very, very, very slowly. Well, you can imagine how that went over with everyone, including me. Gary put it very well when, as we walked down the steps after the play, he said to all of us, "I've... had.... more... fun... at...the...dentist." It was some time before I planned another outing.

Our first car was a gift the summer after we celebrated our third anniversary. Gary had been offered a summer job working as a student engineer at Martin Marietta in Denver. Bikes provided transportation before that time, so we would make trips to the store every few days, and pedal to classes and to movies on Saturday nights. One evening we rode downtown to see Alfred Hitchcock's touted movie, *The Birds*. We loved the suspense of the plot, but you have never seen two people zip home as quickly as we did, periodically glancing around to see if any birds were following. And we still laugh about the time we decided we needed air in the tires. I told Gary that he needed to ask the station attendant how much pressure would be appropriate, but he rejected my pleas only to have the tire eventually explode. This was one of those times that it was more effective for me not to say, "I told you so."

Another one of our pre-car adventures involved a motorbike that Gary rented one afternoon. We had a bit of a fight, about what I have no idea, and he left the house in a huff. An hour or so later, I heard a series of beeps right outside the front windows. Pulling the drapes aside, there sat Gary on a motorbike with a big grin on his face. He had rented it at the gas station and it was ours for the next two hours. When I asked how to operate it, he assured me that he had been given a quick lesson. I think the lesson was too brief because as we drove along the hills, Gary was unable to stop and ended up crashing into a curb. The ride to turn the bike back in was much slower, but it was still in good shape and we were both relieved that our adventure was over long before the bike was due back at the station.

We had a nightly ritual for many, many years that still raises eyebrows when we tell acquaintances about it. From the first year of our marriage, we have taken baths together. When I was growing up, my sister, Susan, and I took baths together. I guess when you are one of six children it's difficult to find "alone time." So our nightly baths provided a chance for the two of us to talk about school, friends, and, later, boy friends. Maybe I was so used to sharing my bath that I convinced Gary that it would be a good idea. We still do this now and then, but with expanding hips and waists, it isn't as easy to do as it once was. On the occasion that we do, however, our ritual has changed. Now candles, music and a glass of wine have been incorporated into bath time together.

In between semesters at Boulder we would take car trips around Colorado. We particularly loved going up Boulder Canyon and often stopped for lunch along the way. The Pie and Eye (real name) was a favorite where we enjoyed homemade pies. One Sunday we set out and spotted a new place that looked like a good possibility for lunch. We seated ourselves and waited, and waited and waited. Finally Gary got up and inquired about their lack of response and was told that we were part of a church retreat. We quietly left, trying hard not to attract more attention than we already had.

We indeed loved our years at Boulder. They were many because Gary went on to earn the MBA and PhD before we took off for central Pennsylvania.

* * *

All seven of the Kochenberger siblings have college degrees; three have advanced degrees, including Gary, so they fully understand the importance of education. My father-in-law, Austin, worked his way up to head of the Shipping Department at the CF&I (the Mill), but he watched many young college graduates pass him by and go on to bigger and better positions. He was somewhat bitter about that, but this bitterness caused him to emphasize the importance of education to his seven children.

A large percentage of the family went into education as a profession. Twenty of us (counting spouses) are or have been preschool, elementary, secondary or college teachers. As the Baptist minister said at the funeral of my father-in-law, "If your children have not yet had one of the Kochenbergers for a teacher, they eventually will."

Many kids grew up having more than one Kochenberger as a teacher. The first year that Gary taught out at the college in our hometown, a young man got on the elevator at the same time he did.

"You know," the student remarked. "I had your brother Kent for gym in junior high, your brother Chuck for physiology when I was in high school and now I have you!"

My sister-in-law, Sandy, also a teacher, and I laughed when one of her first grade students transferred from one school to another in the middle of the school year—from her class to mine. Shawn had no trouble learning my name since his teacher had been another Mrs. Kochenberger. I told his mother that he probably thought that our name was as common as that of Smith and Jones.

Part 2

ANGUISH AND SOLACE

It visits when it chooses, often unexpectedly, always unwanted, always taking over and demanding to have its way without regard for others.
It covers everything black, steals your very spirit, and gives new meaning to vulnerability.
It challenges your ability to cope with adversity like few other illnesses. Those who manage to cope have been tested to the limit. Somehow, they muster the incredible strength and resourcefulness to survive.
For those severely depressed, the minutes, hours and days are a lonely battle between life and death.

-- Gary, March 23, 1997

CHAPTER 8:
Family Ties

Stop worrying about what might have been and focus on what is.

Live each day fully and keep occupied. Be grateful for what I have rather than regret what I don't.

Great advice, but advice I found difficult to follow. Writing it down was helpful because it reinforced how I *should* have been living my life.

THE DIAGNOSIS

They said I had bipolar disorder, also called manic-depressive illness. It was good to finally get a name for it. Sandy said I wasn't a "typical bipolar" though, because I was experiencing lows that were much more dominant than the highs. I would fall hard, as I have described; but during the "highs," when I would feel great, it was more like normalcy than manic. I believe that I have been manic a few times, but it wasn't a common experience.

Experiencing mania is in itself frightening. Those times that I was manic, I would drive too fast, play loud music and talk rapidly. I was very articulate, slept little and even had thoughts of grandeur...for example, believing that I had superior knowledge in many areas, I freely gave people advice, much of which, I am certain, was not welcome.

The naïve hope of complete recovery I'd had the day I left Dr. Carney's office with Sandy's phone number gradually slipped away as I continued to combat my symptoms. I was put on medication and a therapy schedule, but it would be years before I would feel in control of myself for long periods of time.

We would meet with Sandy four more times that first year before the three of us made the decision that I was doing well enough to leave therapy. *Maybe it will never return* was my fervent hope.

But eighteen months later I was back in therapy, having reverted to the symptoms of depression I have come to know so well. I continued to meet with Sandy over the next six years for a total of 71 sessions before we moved to Denver in 1984.

When things were very bad, Sandy and I would meet once a week, then perhaps every other week. I took a preventative approach in that I didn't allow too much time to elapse between sessions, a hard lesson that I learned during those eighteen months. After a year in Denver in 1984-1985, we moved back to State College, and I again saw him on a regular basis until we moved once again to Colorado in 1986.

A FAMILY ILLNESS?

How could a seemingly healthy, happy person suffer such despair? I believe genetics are to blame. As I think back on my years growing up, I now realize that my mother was severely depressed. She spent many days in her bedroom lying down because she had a "migraine." She did have migraine headaches that were brought on by allergies. I remember that she went to Colorado Springs twice a year to see a specialist. He would test her for allergies and she would discover what she was allergic to at that particular time. Then she would avoid it. But it was frustrating for her because these allergies changed. She might be able to eat chocolate when tested at a particular time, only to discover that she was highly allergic to it the next time she was tested. The migraine headaches became so debilitating that she had to go to bed. She would lie in her darkened bedroom for hours, sometimes sleeping the entire day.

I now wonder if that was all that took her away from the rest of the house-hold. I think that depression may have been a factor in her isolation. It may well have been depression that made her moody, so subject to highs and lows. When we were growing up, my sister Susan and I were never able to predict her moods. Sometimes she was happy, other times she was angry or despondent. We would find ourselves taking a "mood check" before we asked to go somewhere or invite a friend to spend the night.

When I returned home for visits with my mother after I was married and had children, she would often lie on the couch for much of the day. She seemed to have no ambition, no desire to do anything other than remain where she was. I remember thinking she was lazy, but once I came to know depression I realized that perhaps it wasn't laziness at all.

My mother's mood swings now became mine, but unlike her, I refused to show them to others. I had hated having to grow up with that unpredictability, waiting until "the time was right" before Susan or I would attempt to ask her permission to do things.

I now think that this was one reason why I kept my depression from my children. I didn't want them to grow up amidst all that uncertainty, listening for the intonation in my voice, always treading lightly and never knowing.

Growing up with my mother's moods made me aware of how an illness can affect an entire family. So, years later, when depression entered my life, I knew I was not the only one who would be affected. My husband's life was turned upside down too as he struggled along beside me. He became much more than my mate. He became the only friend on whom I could rely, the sole parent, not only to our two children, but in a very real sense, to me as well. He became the one and only decision maker, the bookkeeper, and the caretaker of all that a household requires. I needed more care and was the source of more concern than our two children combined. But, despite this almost unbearable burden, he literally and figuratively remained with me, providing me the only bit of sanity that remained. "It was nothing," he later told me, but I know otherwise…

GARY: "I was totally unprepared for the new chapter in our lives. I didn't even know that a new chapter had begun until it was well underway. Over the years I have come to know this scourge called depression. I have seen it turn the most important person in my life inside out and take her to the brink of destruction. I have shared her ups and downs and tried to be by her side, giving support throughout. Yet, I don't know depression like Ann and millions of other sufferers know this illness. Short of being depressed, I doubt that anyone can truly know and appreciate its devastation. Nevertheless, I certainly have a view of what depression is.

"Besides being my wife, Ann is my oldest, closest and dearest friend. We know each other very well. Yet, Ann's early experience with depression went unnoticed by me. In the beginning, her depression was a closely held secret. Ann is incredibly good at putting on a front. At first, because of that perfect façade, I simply didn't see or sense the change that was coming over her. It hadn't yet impacted our relationship in any significant way.

"But, when we would go out, it was clear that she felt awkward around people. When invited to a party, she would often slip away from the crowd and seek solitude in an unoccupied room. On many occasions, I would find her alone in a bedroom, perhaps reading a magazine or just sitting there.

"After a few years into her depression, Ann could scarcely function at all in social settings. She had lost all confidence in herself. I came to realize that whatever was happening was something more than simply second-guessing the choices she had made about her career and the like. This was more than early mid-life musings. It became clear that Ann was in the grip of something powerful—something that had completely taken over and threatened her very ability to survive. And so, for several years, we had virtually no social life. We essentially stopped entertaining and turned down, with a variety of excuses, most invitations that came our way."

SNAPSHOT
State College, Pennsylvania May 1978

Now and then I felt obligated to attend social events. Sometimes my feelings of sadness would lift once I was there and I would begin to feel like my "old self," but many times it remained.

I would attempt conversation, pretending that I was happy and that all was well, but it took much effort to pull this off.

This pretense was very exhausting because my depression took away my self-confidence, my train of thought and my ability to carry on intelligent conversations. Words failed me and I would find myself stammering, so I would retreat to another room, the minutes agonizingly long until it was time to go home. I don't think anyone noticed.

I was happiest at home where I didn't have to pretend...pretend to be happy, pretend to be together, pretend to be "me." The old Ann was missing in action. I missed her terribly. I was terrified...

GARY: "During our antisocial years, I did a lot with our kids. Both children were heavily involved in sports. I would spend hours during the week and on the weekends with them at various events. Ann was always supportive but continued to lead two lives. One life was a front from the children and her friends. Here, Ann was a self-assured, happy, competent person. The other life was the lonely, seemingly hopeless struggle with depression.

"For years, Ann's therapist and I were the only ones who knew of her life with depression. She didn't understand it, she was confused by and ashamed of it, and she was absolutely determined not to let anyone know about it. To this day I marvel at her ability to switch back and forth between two lives.

"She would wake up in the morning in the grips of deep depression and struggle to even get out of bed. She would cry for hours at a time—day in and day out. Yet, if there were a phone call she had to take, she would handle it as if everything was fine. And then, as soon as she got off the phone, she would revert back to her depressed state.

"On her own she wasn't getting any better. Ann's perspective on life became more and more unbalanced. Negative things were given large weight. Positive things received very little recognition at all. Anything in the gray area was interpreted as negative. In fact, Ann came to look for, and expect, the negative. When it wasn't there, it was nevertheless anticipated or invented. She developed a "one-size-fits-all" perspective on life—all negative.

"Given the severity of her depression, our relationship changed considerably over time. For years we had enjoyed an equal partnership. We were lovers, parents and friends. But, as time went on, our relationship slowly became redefined as something quite different. Ann's needs were all-consuming. She could not function as before as a parent or a lover. And, our friendship was getting more and more one-sided. She took and I gave."

CHAPTER 9:
Slipping Away

SNAPSHOT
Denver, Colorado Summer 1984

Each time we moved, I found myself much like Alice in Wonderland tumbling down the rabbit hole. Like Alice, I fell fast, head over heels; and, like her, I had no idea where I was going.

After living in State College for sixteen years, Gary pursued a job opportunity at the University of Denver. We felt that this was a good time for a move because Susan would be graduating from State High and Dave would be entering high school. We knew that we eventually wanted to get back to Colorado to be close to family, and this was the perfect opportunity.

We discussed the move many times...would I be able to handle it? Knowing my mental history caused us to "proceed with caution." We did a two-sided chart, writing down pros and cons (we would get very proficient at these). In the end, we decided to do it. We were all excited about this new adventure that lay ahead.

I did everything I could to prepare myself for this change. I spent a couple of months making a scrapbook about State College for each child. I took pictures of all the schools they had attended, of Holmes Foster Park, the favorite pizza hangout and the arcade where Dave and his friends had frequented. In the front of each scrapbook was a long poem, telling of their years growing up in this small town. They were delighted and the entire project had been therapeutic for me.

We left for Denver in July of 1984. I remember that the summer was hot, and the house we had rented had a family room in back that the late afternoon sun heated up each day. Being the frugal person I am, I didn't think it was necessary to run the air conditioner very much, so we sweltered. Dave made friends with a nice boy who was a year older and lived across the street. Greg introduced him to a variety of kids, so he had school friends even before school started. Susan started at the University of Denver as a freshman, pledged Delta Gamma and loved the college experience. She played on the tennis team and did excellent work academically. Gary loved his new position and was enjoying his colleagues. Everyone was happy, including me...but, after just three weeks, that happiness slipped out of my grasp.

It came from out of nowhere, that unwelcome visitor. I can identify nothing specific that led to that first major breakdown, but I guessed it was the fact that I was adjusting to so many changes. After I fell, everything bothered me—everything—so we moved at the end of that year. And then we moved at the end of the next year...constantly packing, moving and unpacking, all because of me.

That first move had been a professional one for Gary, but the next two moves were due to my collapsed state of mind. I simply was not able to adjust, let alone cope where I was. In Denver, I was miserable. Seeing me so unhappy, Gary tried to find a way to get us back to Pennsylvania. He flew out to talk to the dean at Penn State and got offered a job there. So back we moved in the summer of 1985.

But was I happy then? Far from it. I became more and more frantic about the idea of moving *back* to Colorado, knowing that it was the depression that had been behind all of this discontent, but also knowing that all I wanted to do was to alleviate some of the mental anguish I was experiencing. You think you will be happier if you go elsewhere. I wanted to recapture where we left off in Denver, to put myself back in time as if we had never left, but happiness is not possible when depression is present. They cannot coexist. I thought they could, but they can't. Then, once you grasp some idea of reality and recognize that all that you thought would bring happiness does not, it's too late.

But the early years at State College *had* been wonderful...

WINTER WONDERLAND IN THE EAST

The memories stick with me to this day. Especially holidays. I have always loved holidays, so our little family developed many customs around them. When we couldn't travel to Colorado to celebrate Christmas with the families, I would plan special treats with Susan and Dave. We would make gingerbread houses, host cookie decorating parties and cross-country ski on the Penn State golf course. We would arrive home, bodies aching from the bitter cold and humid Pennsylvania air, and make cups of hot chocolate the "old fashioned way"...no packets for us. We'd sit around our wonderful Vermont Castings wood-burning stove in our family room and talk about how many more days we had to wait until Christmas.

Dave has always been a very early riser, so he would be up at painfully early hours on Christmas morning, stand by our bedside and continually inquire, "When can we have breakfast and open our presents?" We would eventually give up and get up, and would soon be enjoying the traditional Christmas coffee cake I made each year as Dave passed the gifts. Gary, Susan and I never had to worry because Dave took charge...we just sat, ate and opened.

After years of being coaxed out of bed far too early, I had a wonderful idea that continued each year after. Susan and Dave were allowed to see what was in their stockings before we got up, so I packed his full of receipt books, pens, hole punchers, stickers and anything else that might keep him busy. He spent enough time playing with all of his goodies that we were able to catch a few more ZZZs before finding him beside our bed, receipt book in hand and pencil poised, ready to take our order for breakfast.

One year I read that there would be a Christmas concert at one of the campus auditoriums and thought that it would be good for all of us to attend the program. Despite a bit of groaning from Gary and the two kids, we settled into our seats to listen to the Christmas music. I think Susan must have been eight and Dave was probably five.

Anyone sitting behind us would have thought that there was an empty space where Dave was sitting because he was so small. At some point during the concert, he started to "expel a little gas." This went on for much of the performance. Gary, worried that people might think that he was the one making such noises, made certain that Dave's presence was obvious.

As we walked from the concert to the car, we discussed the evening and I remarked that it had been enjoyable. Gary turned to Dave as he said, "And we enjoyed the tuba concert that you provided, Dave."

We still remember that, and laugh about it from time to time.

At the end of one summer Colorado visit, we purchased cross-country skis for the four of us and drove back to Pennsylvania with them. We used them often over Christmas breaks. We would dress in layers because it can be so bitter cold and would then head up to the university to ski around the golf course. Cross-country skiing is a great form of exercise because your upper body gets a workout as well as your lower body. By the time we got back to the car, many of our layers of clothing would be tied around our waists because your body heats up quickly.

I remember that during one particularly severe storm, I decided to put on my skis and ski around the schoolyard that was just down the hill from our backyard. As was often the case, however, it was icy and I got only a few paces before I found myself on my back. I immediately took off my skis and went back into the house.

The snow in the East is not at all like it is in Colorado. Because of the humidity, it is never dry or light in weight, and it is harder to sled or ski. The school kids would sled down the sidewalk that led to the school and were able to sled for hours once the snow was packed down. I can remember Susan and Dave arriving home from their outdoor adventures, freezing cold, but smiling.

Before the two of them were old enough to go to school, our days together were idyllic. We loved going to the library where they were allowed twelve books each (library rule). We'd browse and carefully select, check out and head for the couch once we arrived home. Because I had always read to them often, both kids loved books. We would read in the afternoons and again before bedtime. We'd paint, color and work puzzles by the hour. We'd often bake cookies together, especially for Christmas and Valentine's Day. For birthdays, we created cakes in the shape of a sailboat, a witch or a train. I have passed down the Baker's Coconut booklet to Susan, its yellowed, dog-eared pages indicating years of use.

Occasions of any sort were cause for celebration at our house. I always left a small present on the bed of each child for them to open when they came home on that last day of the school year. It was a celebration of a job well done. Summers were filled with swimming, visits to the parks and carefree days...lemonade stands, garage sales and playing with friends.

The Central Pennsylvania Festival of the Arts, or The Arts Festival as everyone refers to it, is held for a week in the middle of July. It's great fun...vendors sell jewelry, pottery and art; plays are held on campus, music groups play on street corners and the food is wonderful. Throughout all the years we lived in State College, we witnessed the Festival increase in both quality and quantity.

There was always a small section set aside at which young entrepreneurs were able to sell their creations. Things like jewelry, stationary and small toys could be found displayed on tables. Susan was about nine when she and her friend across the street, Wendy Skipper, decided that they wanted to be involved. Soon after the first of the year, they began to create "Pom Pom People," figures made with small pom poms doing a variety of activities. Tennis, winter sports and swimming as well as various other themes were depicted. In the hot summer sun, the two girls sat sweating under large umbrellas as we brought thermoses filled with iced water to prevent them from getting heat stroke. Temperatures are unusually hot in July; sometimes they reach the mid-nineties, so sitting in the heat all day is no easy task.

The idea turned out to be a great success...each girl cleared $79.00 after expenses that first year. Susan was proud of her accomplishment and we knew that entire project had been a wonderful learning experience. I remember that she bought a hooded winter coat and a comforter for her bed with the proceeds. The two young businesswomen continued selling various creations for a few more years before "retiring" from their summer project.

We would drive to Colorado for a couple of weeks each July to go on the Kochenberger family fishing trip and to see all of the grandparents, aunts, uncles and cousins. It was our way to keep up with the family from which we lived so far. It wasn't the same as living among all of them, but it was the second best thing.

We drove those 1,650 miles from Pennsylvania to Colorado for years. That was during the time before air conditioning and speed limits over 50 mph, so it took two nights on the road and half a day of day three before we would arrive...drenched and exhausted from the hot car. Our first trip back to Colorado occurred five months after we had moved to Pennsylvania the first time. Gary had an opportunity to teach at the University of Colorado that summer so we threw what was necessary into the car, Dave traveling in one of those car beds and Susan in her car seat.

There was so much in the back seat that Susan looked at Gary and asked, "Daddy, where do I sit?"

"Right there," he told her as he pointed to the car seat in the middle of boxes piled high. "There's lots of room."

Even a three and a half year old is able to recognize lots of room. She quickly retorted, "That's not lots of room."

With hot wind blowing in our faces we set out and each time we stopped I would pick up my three-month-old son, being careful that his sweaty body didn't slip out of my hands.

A year or two later, Dave brought along a toy horn on the trip, something we didn't discover until he loudly blew it from the back seat. Gary's head nearly hit the roof. He thought it was a semi blasting its horn behind us. Everyone laughed but Gary, who told Dave to "put that damn horn away."

To pass the hours, we'd sing songs, look for license plates from different states and play the alphabet billboard game. We'd play twenty questions and sometimes I would remember to purchase games and books specifically written for long road trips. Two memorable trips stand out...one was when Dave, having a severe case of diarrhea, caused us to make eighteen bathroom stops between home and the Pennsylvania border. (Being one who keeps track of things, particularly those incidences having to do with numbers, yes, I counted.) Another time our BMW broke down a couple of hours from State College. Gary got out, looked under the hood as if he knew what he was doing (he didn't) and discovered a loose wire, which he hooked up with one of those wire twist things that are used to close the end of bread bags. The car managed to go the rest of the way to Colorado, only to give out on Main Street close to midnight in our hometown of Pueblo. His older brother Kent, a car enthusiast, just shook his head.

We sold the car the next day and drove home with a brand new VW station wagon *with* air conditioning. It wasn't the air conditioning we enjoy today, but it helped make our return trip through the humidity of Nebraska, Iowa and Ohio much more bearable.

* * *

But all the moves took a toll on all of us. Thank heavens for our family's sense of humor. Sometimes it would surface when least expected...

One day, at the end of Dave's junior year (it was 1987, our third move in so many years, and we were living in Pueblo at this point), Gary and I were sitting at the kitchen table, eating dinner with him. Dave looked at us with that dimpled smile across his face and asked, "Well, where will I be for my senior year?" The three of us had a good laugh despite the fact that we also realized that there was sadness and regret in the statement as well.

And Gary? One day after we had been in Pueblo a while, he said to me, "You know I was driving to work this morning and I was looking out at the prairie...the desert-like plants and the prairie dog mounds..."

I just *knew* what was coming next. I knew that he was going to say that he hated it here, that he hated the fact that he was going to this university rather than the Penn State campus he had so loved.

Instead he said, "You know, it is so beautiful. There is such beauty in the desert flowers, especially those purple ones. And the prairie dogs are so numerous and playful. I love watching them dart about."

This is so like Gary...so positive...so seeing the good rather than the bad, the light rather than the dark. This was so me when I was well, but it was the Other Ann that he was living with now.

When incredulous family and friends questioned why we left Penn State and returned to Pueblo ("Another move...why?"), he would calmly answer, "We left because of family. We wanted to be with family and we had this opportunity to do so."

Of course we *had* left for family—the wife he lived with. But having the extended family around all of us was a wonderful thing at a time when we so needed the support that only loved ones are able to provide.

It was a double-edged sword that Gary was able to go from one university to another so easily. Because he is well known and has a wonderful resume, he is very marketable. This asset, however, may have been a liability because, had we stayed put in Denver after that first move (1984), I would have eventually adjusted. I was beginning to adjust at the time that we moved back to Pennsylvania the following year and I believe that would have continued. But retrospect is a rather useless exercise.

Living among family in Pueblo was just what we needed in 1986. Gary was hired as department chair in the College of Business at The University of Southern Colorado, later renamed Colorado State University at Pueblo when our state system was revamped.

This was high school number three for Dave as he began his junior year at Central, the school from which my father and all of my siblings and I graduated. My brother-in-law, Chuck Kochenberger, was a member of the high school faculty. Chuck had hopes of being a sort of mentor to Dave, steering him in the right direction. Dave, however, goes his own way so when he did follow Chuck's suggestions it was not because his uncle had told him to do so, but because Dave had chosen to do so. Uncle Chuck was there when Dave needed lunch money, could talk him into writing out an excuse when he was late to class as well as when he wanted to just touch base with him.

This was a difficult adjustment for Dave, but his ability to make friends easily was in his favor. Since his shoulder injury prevented him from considering the wrestling team, he was able to play on the first soccer team the high school put into place that year.

YET ANOTHER PSYCHOLOGIST

Predictably, another move meant instability for me. As many benefits as there were to this move back to our hometown, I am predisposed to be negatively affected. It was great being with my mother and younger brother, Bob, as well as with Gary's family. We were able to be more involved in the lives of our young nieces and nephews, attending dance recitals and sporting events.

But I continued to ruminate over the fact that I was solely responsible for our having left Denver the year before, and the school year in Pennsylvania had been extremely difficult on my mental health. The many moves were taking their toll, so my family doctor suggested I see a therapist.

Carole Crawford turned out to be an excellent recommendation. Our sessions were beneficial, and unquestionably provided a psychological boost when I desperately needed one. As I regained confidence in getting through the day, my return to the teaching profession was quite successful, in large due to my work with Carole. Gary, Dave and I had family sessions as well and I know that Dave was able to begin to understand the reasons behind our nomadic way of life.

WHY ALL THE MOVES?

Well, useless exercise or not, I have to say the 1985 move back to Pennsylvania from Colorado had been a huge mistake. It was a mistake, though, that can be logically justified. Anyone in the midst of severe depression just wants to get out. I had often been happy in State College and I believed that it was there that I would find happiness once again. I didn't realize then that my happiness was dependent on what was happening internally rather than externally.

Because unfamiliarity is so stressful when you are depressed, I believed that State College would provide the feeling of being comfortable that was missing. New places mean a new home, new doctors, new everything...school, work, cleaners, gas station. It was a constant search for the first several months and this was the time period when the move affected me the most.

In Denver, I always had a litany of excuses why I should leave. I was used to State College, where everyone knew everyone else. It was a short drive anywhere in town. The university was seven minutes away by car or bike. Even Sandy's office had been just blocks away.

In Denver, drives were long. I commuted to work, something I had never done. It took me thirty minutes, and the drive was horrific. It seemed I was always in the midst of hundreds of people and all of this caused my anxiety to skyrocket.

Lines were long, houses were close together in a sea of rooftops on hillsides, and traffic moved way too fast. In Pennsylvania, deciduous trees were everywhere so it was not possible to see for long distances because the trees blocked the view. Not so in the West, and this *really* bothered me. I hated the wide-open spaces, the lack of foliage and the bright sun. I hated the crowds, the unfamiliarity of the streets and the fact that I had left all my friends behind. (Note: it is now 2006 and I am back in Denver and I love it.)

CHAPTER 10:
Striving to Survive

SNAPSHOT
Back in State College again September 1985

I am substitute teaching fifth grade today. The kids run up and down the soccer field, as I sit beside it. I am in severe pain and feel wired, as if I am one constant electrical charge.

I thought my depression in Denver last year was my worst episode, but, clearly, this current one surpasses it.

I am so empty and life is so difficult that I think I will kill myself when I get home this afternoon. This would be best for everyone, especially me. I know where the bottles are, on the middle shelf of the linen closet. I have others from Denver so I am sure that it is enough. I can see all the pills in bottles in the linen closet.

I feel better now. I feel tremendous relief knowing that I have made this decision.

This living hell will soon be over.

I vividly remember that afternoon on the soccer field. I was *almost happy* the rest of the day. Somewhere between the time I made this decision and the time I arrived back home, however, I changed my mind. I had gained some sense of control, my death wish was over and I believed I *would* be able to cope once again. And then, the phone had rung as I walked in the door and Gary had arrived soon after and began telling me about his day. So, for that day anyway, I put the suicide thoughts aside, but I knew it was an option if I chose not to continue to live.

Strangely, the thought of ending my life made the severe depression more tolerable. It seems paradoxical, but it makes perfect sense. Suicide is the ultimate coping strategy...knowing that I have a way to get out of the pain gives me a sense of relief and comfort. I always know that if my life gets too painful, ending it is a way out. While I am not able to control any other part of my life, I know I can choose to end it. This results in a feeling of empowerment and that emotion is a positive one that enables me to have the strength to continue to fight the demon.

The summer of 1985 when we returned to State College from Denver had been an excruciating one. Not only did I realize that we should never have returned and should have continued to adjust to our new life in Denver, I also was wracked by guilt because I had disrupted the lives of our entire family. It is a terrifying realization that you are responsible for changing the direction—negatively—in which everyone else is headed. Thoughts would race through my mind and I would feel panic and experience cold sweats as I watched my children try to readjust to the old lives they thought they had left behind forever.

Neither Susan nor Dave had wanted to leave Denver. They had new friends and they loved their schools. Susan had no adjustment period at the University of Denver and exhulted in friends, sorority and her classes. Gary was able to watch her tennis team at practice every afternoon since the Business School was just across the street from the courts. Dave's adjustment when first coming to Denver had taken a while, as you would expect for normal kids, but he was fine. Gary enjoyed his colleagues and his faculty position, and I know that it was hard for him to turn in his resignation at the University of Denver, but I was his priority.

But now that we were back in Pennsylvania it was agonizing for me to watch my children adjust once again. Each time I saw unhappiness in Susan's eyes or witnessed Dave struggle to "fit in" after being away from his childhood friends for a year, my heart would break. Guilt would overwhelm me, and I would hate myself for doing this to them. What kind of a mother was I? Why couldn't I help them rather than destroy their lives? I was responsible for their unhappiness.

DAVE: "I remember first noticing a difference in my mom's behavior when we moved to Denver in 1984. I was fourteen and was just starting high school. I vividly remember finding her after school, sitting up in her bed trying to hide her emotions. Her eyes were red and swollen from constant crying and the room was littered with wet tissues. She tried to assure me that everything was all right, but I knew something was wrong. I didn't understand why this was so difficult for my mom.

"I was told the reason we moved to Denver at that time was because my dad's father, my Grandpa Austin, had by-pass surgery. Although it was difficult for me to leave my world in Pennsylvania after eighth grade, I understood that my dad wanted to be closer to his father.

"Ninth grade was challenging for me. I dislocated my shoulder in December. As a result, my ability to compete in sports was taken away. My identity was becoming clouded at a very impressionable time in my life, and adjusting to a new school was difficult.

"Meanwhile, I kept asking my mom what I could do to help. My parents kept telling me that everything was fine, but I knew that something was wrong. I started to wonder if it was something that I had done. I knew that my mom wasn't doing well, but I had no idea why. It just didn't seem right that she was so upset about leaving Pennsylvania.

"When my parents told me that we were moving back to Pennsylvania, I couldn't believe my ears. I was happy because I would be going back to my world and everything would be all right. I was headed back to my roots and mom would be fine.

"Three months after we returned to State College, I dislocated my shoulder again. My dad and I visited several doctors for advice. We decided to try rehab one more time, but several months later, the shoulder popped out again. We opted for surgery that April of 1986. Three months later, I was able to remove the sling from my shoulder and begin rehab the third time. I had just finished nineteen months of physical and mental pain and suffering.

And then the reality of moving back to Colorado set in. Due to my immature age, I was really resentful toward my dad. I felt that he pushed me to rehab my shoulder over and over again just so I could compete in sports.

"I had no way of comprehending what my mom was going through. Therefore, I couldn't understand why my parents kept moving me across the country. "My mom did a great job of masking her depression. In, fact, she was a master at it. So why were we moving back to Colorado again? Why did I have to go through this again? It's extremely difficult to adjust to new high schools. It takes at least a year to make new friends, especially when you are not involved in sports. This was my third school in three years and for what?

"Grandpa Austin was doing better, and if we had moved back to Pennsylvania we must not have been too concerned about his health. I was extremely angry.

"The fall of 1986 was the most difficult time for me. In fact after moving my mom out to Colorado, I made my dad drive to Pennsylvania to pick me up. I didn't say a word to him for the entire 1,600 miles."

"PROMISE ME"

And in the midst of all this internal turmoil that hot summer in 1985, Gary arrived home from the university one day, ran to me, put his head down and broke down. I was stunned. He tried to tell me what he was so upset about, but it took some time until he calmed down. He told me that the wife of one of his colleagues had taken her own life the night before.

"Promise me that you will never, never do that to us. Promise me," he pleaded in between gasps. I promised him, and, at that moment, I emphatically meant what I said.

Recollections such as this often would come back to me during those times when I seriously thought of ending my life. I would see Gary coming home from the university that afternoon, running to me...the entire scene replays, and remains in my mind long enough that I rethink my plans. I am reminded that my husband and my children must be considered when I make decisions for myself because those decisions will affect not only me.

But believing that this is true...and I truly believe that it is...is simply not enough to put aside constant thoughts of suicide. All I wanted was to end the agony, and ending it forever is a very desirable enticement.

I told myself many times that, although I believed Gary, Susan and Dave would be far better off without me, they didn't believe the same. In my depressive state, I was convinced that they were wrong, but because *I had promised*, I had to keep my word.

Promises have always been sacred to me. Thinking back to my childhood, it was my mother who always told us that a promise is never, never to be broken. This belief has always been etched in my mind and is something I have stressed to my children.

My father, as a physician, had seen many people commit suicide and once remarked that it was "the coward's way out." This made absolutely no sense to me at the time. Surely it takes more courage to kill yourself rather than not to, but of course, that was before I became ill. Then I discovered that he was right. It takes far more courage to stay in a living hell within the twisted thoughts that occupy the mind of the depressed than it does to commit suicide.

My father had experienced depression firsthand. He was sent home from active duty during World War II, suffering from mental illness following his attempt to save two drowning pilots off the coast of the Philippines. He was the only man in his unit who swam well enough to attempt the rescue, but he managed to save only one of the men. It was the screams of the one he had to leave behind that were the reason for his mental breakdown.

After months of sitting up nights because he was unable to sleep, losing many pounds because he could no longer eat, the Army sent my father home. My Grandfather Baker met him in Utah and he was in an Army mental facility there for eight months.

Following his release, he worked for a year at the Colorado State Hospital because his father knew the head psychiatrist, and because it was a "safe" place for him to be. My mother told me that she had to walk to work with him each morning because he couldn't do it without her. It took a long time before he recovered.

I have never believed that my depression is linked to my father. His breakdown was due to severe stress, something that was completely understandable and certainly not unexpected given the situation that he endured. His depression never reoccurred.

But his long recovery is certainly familiar to me. All three of my major episodes required many, many months of recovery, the one that would occur in 2000 much longer. Confidence and self-esteem are gone. These are not easy to rebuild when you have fallen so far downward. They return very slowly... one step forward and two steps back, as they say. You think that things might be normal once again, but something happens that quickly reminds you that recovery is still a long way away. Taking that one step forward is easy to do when everything is running smoothly, but when something goes wrong or I would receive negative comments or news, my reaction is an accurate assessment of my mental stability.

THE TRUTH ABOUT SUICIDE

Because people still don't talk about suicide a lot, I think this needs stressing: Before I experienced this illness, I was of the opinion that the reason mentally ill people didn't act on their thoughts of suicide was because they didn't want to hurt those left behind. I now know otherwise. It is precisely for that reason that you *believe you should*. I was convinced that my family would be far better off without me because I was disrupting their lives in such a big way. Oh, I knew they would be devastated when I was gone, but I thought they would eventually recover and have a much better life without me in it. Of course I was wrong, but rationality and depression cannot coexist.

I also believe that no one can prevent anyone from committing suicide if that person is determined to end his or her life. Relatives of suicide victims experience tremendous guilt and regret that they "missed obvious signs." Yet no one can be with another person twenty-four hours a day. If the person is determined to commit suicide, he or she *will* succeed. And while someone else may convince you that you should not give up, it's possible to feel otherwise, even a few hours later. The back and forth...should I? shouldn't I?...is something with which those of us with this dreadful illness have to constantly contend. It is exhausting.

So, if someone you know who is severely depressed tells you they have never thought about suicide, don't believe it for a minute. There is no way that it does not enter the minds of those who suffer this illness. I would assume one of three things...either the person is not being honest, does not want to reveal this fact or he or she isn't severely depressed.

Family members left behind often make the comment that although their loved one had been despondent, he or she had "seemed so happy" of late. I was happy too when I decided to commit suicide because I knew that my suffering would soon end. I am certain that this is the reason for such behavior changes in many who suffer from depression.

In addition to merely thinking about ending my life, I thought about specific plans. All involved medication...antidepressants, Xanax, any medication I had on hand. I knew that I had to have a sufficient amount of pills available because the last thing I wanted to do was to *almost* complete my plan. With the exception of one time, I never went beyond obsessing about the idea and picturing myself waiting to be alone, collecting the pills, going into the bathroom and swallowing all of them at once.

The thinking of those who are depressed is neither rational nor clear. You are often paranoid and the world around you is distorted. What becomes obviously apparent once the darkness leaves is anything but obvious at the time depression is present. When in the midst of it, my reality is all of these things, but it is my reality.

GARY: "The one area where Ann continued to function fairly normally was with respect to our kids. But, while she continued to put on a front for them, I had assumed most of the parenting duties. This was especially true with any important decisions that had to be made.

"When Ann would wake up depressed, regardless of the pain and the feelings of hopelessness, she would hide it from the kids. I came to recognize the depression quite easily and would do what I could to help her get started with the day. Sometimes we would talk for hours at a time. By being patient and talking about her feelings, I hoped she could change her perspective. We would talk endlessly about trying to have a balanced view of life, about all the positive things we had in our lives and about the many blessings we had.

"Ann would often say the right things, as if trying to please me. The emptiness in her eyes and voice told a different story.

"During our many discussions, I became a devoted confidant and lay counselor. By now she was getting regular professional help and was taking various medications. Nevertheless, we continued our frequent talks about her state of mind. I had my limitations as a counselor. My background was in engineering, mathematics and business. I had no formal training in psychology. I did, however, have pretty good listening skills and a large supply of patience. The latter, however, as large as it was, became tested at times. I worried constantly about Ann and whether or not she could find the courage and the will to deal with what was happening to her. I felt frustrated about this major discontinuity in our lives and I was very much afraid of where it might be leading.

"We never explicitly spoke about suicide, but we both knew it was an option. Ann's desperate state and the availability of pills and other means of self-destruction made this a possibility I couldn't ignore. When she was having a bad day, I would make unexpected phone calls. On many occasions I would drive home in the middle of the day for a surprise visit, or I would invite her to meet me for lunch. Despite such efforts, the opportunity of this final act remained part of our lives and I worried constantly that her last day would come.

"Faced with little knowledge of depression or psychology, I read several so called self-help books. The two of us had read many books recommended by her therapists over the years so these were around the house. As new books came to our attention, we would both read them and add them to our collection. We would discuss the things that we had learned. Even today, storage room boxes or infrequently used drawers often contain some of these books—grim reminders of the past.

"In general, I found such books to be useful. They gave us a common language and a set of concepts and notions to discuss and try to relate to what we were experiencing. Unfortunately, they offered no definitive solutions to the problems we faced. The business of depression is far too complicated for that.

"In the beginning, I had doubts about the value of counseling—doubts based upon ignorance about what it really entailed. Today, I recognize how important it is and how much a competent therapist can serve as a catalyst in the coping/recovery process. Counseling certainly played a key role in Ann's recovery. My role was decidedly different.

"At times, I would try to introduce variations into our daily discussions. Sometimes new themes maybe even new challenges. In spite of my good intentions, most of these efforts reflected my naiveté. Things are oh so much clearer with hindsight!

"For a while, I was big on the notion that we must take responsibility for our own happiness. I asked our daughter, Susan, to make a brightly colored poster that said "Happy Thoughts Make Happy People." Covered with magnets, this poster was attached to our refrigerator as a reminder for all. I believe to this day that we must, indeed, take responsibility for our own happiness.

"I also believe in the importance of positive thinking—that happy thoughts do, in fact, contribute to making people happy. But, such sloganeering is best suited as gentle reminders for those who might be a bit down. It is far too simplistic to serve as a cure for the deeply depressed. What had a hold of Ann was orders of magnitudes more controlling and far more serious than simply being a bit down. No amount of sloganeering was going to do the trick.

"For the most part, I approached our discussion about Ann's problems in a calm and patient manner. There were times, though, when anger overtook me—I wanted to shake her and tell her to snap out of her self pity, times when I wanted to tell her that I missed the life we had before and that I wanted the 'old' Ann back.

"It was during one of these "mad-as-hell" moments when, quite unexpectedly, something happened that forever solidified my commitment to the calm, patient approach. I was flipping through the TV channels and happened to see a non-denominational public service announcement sponsored by a consortium of churches. The full message, which was about helping one another, has long escaped me. The part that is forever recorded in my mind is, 'Love never quits, love never gives up.' This simple message hit me hard at a time when I most needed it. I will never forget it. It became my mantra.

"Over the years I have repeated these words hundreds, perhaps thousands, of times. They serve as the gentle voice of reason and compassion whenever my patience is about to run short. This simple saying sustained me through many difficult times. Despite the many useful things I learned from the books we read about depression and the therapy sessions I attended, nothing helped me more to help Ann than that simple message I received from TV that day. From that time on, I can't remember ever showing anything but compassion and understanding towards her struggle. I often had angry thoughts, but they were never communicated to Ann."

* * *

Neither Gary nor I have ever mentioned the word "suicide" to each other. It is, I think, a horrifying word. It even looks horrifying when seen in print. I was afraid that mentioning the word might bring me closer to it; I was too close as it was, so it never became a part of my vocabulary.

The faces of Susan and David would flash in my mind during down times. I would see their laughter, and then their tears, and I would rethink my plan. I would have endured *any* amount of pain before I would allow any harm to come to them. In essence, that was what I did.

But in June of 2000, something happened to change that resolve.

CHAPTER 11:
The Last Move

In 1999 Gary was given the opportunity to establish a research center at the University of Mississippi. We were now living in our own home in the Denver area. Susan had married John in 1991 and lived nearby. I had obtained a masters degree and was still teaching. I was feeling fine.

Gary's position would allow him to work with companies on production problems. It was something about which he felt both honored and excited. He would have the freedom, along with the funding, to bring his expertise to the building of the center. His only reservation was me, the albatross...would this move be detrimental to my mental health, now tenuously under control?

SHOULD WE OR SHOULDN'T WE?

Trying very hard to be objective, we weighed both sides of the question of moving. Should we go, or should we pass up the opportunity? We discussed this not only with one another, but also with Susan and Dave and with our primary care physician in Denver.

We went back and forth, unable to decide. Given that you are not able to predict, and can only look at things as they currently stand, it is very difficult to make that type of decision. We had *many* pros and cons. And so, we sat down and made yet another list, giving much thought to every aspect of what might potentially trigger a depressive episode.

PRO'S –

1. Living temporarily in the South, an area of the country to which we had never been, would be an adventure.

2. I would get some time off because I would be taking a two-year leave from my school district.

3. I could fly to Denver as often as I wanted to see our children and Susan and John's toddler, our first grandchild, Max.

4. We could rent our home so that we would be able to come back to it two years later.

5. Family could visit from time to time.

That list sounded so wonderful that there seemed to be no reason not to go. We would be crazy to pass up such an opportunity. But then we made the Cons list.

CON'S –

1. I knew that I would miss Max terribly, and that seeing him now and then was not the same thing as seeing him frequently.

2. Would moving, even for two years, actually bring on another depression as it had in the past? History was against us.

3. It was unlikely that I would be able to teach the same grade or even at the same school once my leave was over and I returned.

4. How would I do without the familiarity of our house and our neighborhood?

Our family doctor advised against our move. He had been a part of my recovery during the times I had depressive bouts and knew my vulnerabilities. But...but, it would only be a temporary move, and knowing that we would be coming back to our house and that I was not tied down...well, we were certain that we knew better. We were wrong. We should have listened, but sometimes the thought of adventure and new challenges wins out.

Much more important in my mind was that I very much wanted this for Gary. He had sacrificed so much for me over the past twenty-five years. A conversation with my mother years earlier came back to me...

SNAPSHOT Pueblo, Colorado Spring 1987

My mother and I are sitting in our living room on Carlile Avenue in Pueblo.

She looks at me as she says, "I know that you won't always be here. An opportunity will come along for Gary that he may want to take. You must let him do that if he really wants to because he has done so much for you."

One more item for the pro's side. Besides, I was feeling wonderful, and had experienced no depressive symptoms for the past six or seven years. Why wouldn't I be able make this temporary move? I finally convinced myself that I could. Every conceivable objection was laid to rest before we drove from Colorado to Mississippi that June.

LOVIN' THAT SOUTHERN HOSPITALITY

We purchased a home in Oxford and all was well for many months. We made friends and enjoyed our small town. We loved experiencing the cultural differences as we tried to decipher the southern drawl. I was "Miss A-yon" to those who came to the house to set up cable TV, repair windows or clean carpets. We hired a lawn service, whose owner attempted to educate me on the foliage with which I was not familiar. We had two beautiful bushes filled with huge flowers that sat alongside our driveway. I inquired as to what they were.

He informed me, "Those are crep *muddle*." I asked him to repeat the name, but was once again unable to make sense of what he was saying. I was certain that it must be a type of foliage unfamiliar to me, only to later learn that the bushes were crepe myrtle.

Once a week, I volunteered in a second grade class in the Oxford School District and twice a week at Leap Frog, an after-school remedial reading and math program. Approximately twenty-four children from second and third grade classes were bussed from the school to the church where classes were held.

Most of the volunteers were students from Ole Miss who were fulfilling part of the community service that was required by their fraternities and sororities. The students with whom I interacted were wonderful young people who, like me, were glad to be a part of providing assistance to the kids.

I thought I had a handle on just how different things were in the South until the afternoon I saw a sign on the church door. As I walked closer, it became apparent that Leap Frog was not in session. Puzzled, I knew it was not a holiday. The sign explained that Leap Frog would not be in session that day due to the "impending storm." I had no idea that we would be getting a "storm," but a bit of snow was possible.

"Wow," I thought, "in Colorado things close *after* the storm, not before."

Stopping at the grocery store on the way home, I discovered that shelves were nearly empty as everyone in town was in a panic, stocking up for the expected snowstorm.

Three to four inches fell that Tuesday evening, closing Ole Miss. No one was going anywhere. I even received a call that evening from someone we had invited to a party that was to be held at our home four days later. She said they might not be able to come because of the "storm."

Gary and I loved seeing the four inches that had piled on our deck, reminding us of home. Our dog loved tunneling through the snow in the back yard. But we found it rather ludicrous that these Southern folks were making such a big deal of this little bit of white stuff. I soon realized, though, that many of them had never seen snow, but they sure had been through ice storms that were unlike anything I could have imagined in Colorado. All thoughts of the ridiculousness of all of this quickly reminded me that it's all what you're used to and they weren't used to snow.

AH, MISSISSIPPI

The nearby woods were covered with trees, bushes and ponds, the downtown square was quaint and Ole Miss was a lovely campus. One time we stayed at an enchanting place, the Cedar Grove Antebellum Bed and Breakfast on the Mississippi River in Vicksburg. During a morning tour of the mansion we heard about the hole in the wall near the piano that a cannon ball fired by the Union Army from the Mississippi River had created. It had just missed the head of the man playing that piano that night. The river, the mansion and the beautifully flowered grounds vividly brought that era back to life. For me, it was as if I was in the midst of it, and I was reveling in all of it.

As both a student and a lover of history, I was fascinated with the area and especially the battlefield. It was here that the Battle of Vicksburg had occurred during the Civil War. The battlefield itself was vast, something for which I was not prepared. As we drove through, we saw large stone monuments honoring the men from various units from states throughout the country. Small hills abounded, and I could envision Union or Confederate troops approaching one another over those hills, more than a century and a half ago. It was as if time had not passed and I was a witness to all that had occurred there during the worst war in the history of America.

It is understandable why I, as a history buff, was simply thriving in the South. Living in an area in which so much of the action took place to shape our country emphasizes the fact that I was more than happy in Mississippi...I was loving it. We put the thought of the "cons" of our move there out of our mind. The pros ruled. We had Thanksgiving visitors, our kids flew in often and I did get to fly to Colorado several times.

But a nagging uneasiness first appeared in late April, soon after we had returned from a trip to California to meet my son's future in-laws. Judy and Jack Rebholtz are wonderful people. We got along with them very well and were pleased with the family of which our son, now age 30, would soon be a part. The uneasiness I was beginning to feel was soon replaced with periods of feeling down, then feeling good, only to dip down again. I had not experienced such mood swings for several years. The medication I had been taking for some time was apparently losing its effectiveness. This sometimes happened and alternative medications would be prescribed. Our doctor in Oxford suggested I try a new one, Celexa, so I was once again faced with yet another "medication adjustment period" and braced myself for the expected ups and downs that come with the territory as dosage is adjusted and readjusted. I was certain that my mood would improve once the dosage was sufficient. The mood improvement never came.

ONE MOVE TOO MANY!

Several weeks after our return from our California visit, the bottom fell out. "Feeling down" soon became full-blown depression that was worsening by the day as I fought to grasp my sanity.

JOURNAL ENTRY
Oxford, Mississippi May 15, 2000

I had a very bad night, only sleeping about three hours, lying there until Gary's alarm sounded. I have to make myself eat and drink lots of water.

No wonder I've lost so much weight. I have no appetite... stomach problems may account for this. Then again, this is how I am when depression returns.

I can do this! I can do this! It is incredibly hard right now. I have the classic symptoms of depression...fear, negativity, no energy and, once again, no joy.
Time creeps by.

I took a twenty-five minute walk this morning and am trying to keep busy. Gary is in Salt Lake until Tuesday. I stopped by church and prayed. Things were better as the day wore on, but the day was very long.

Did errands, knitted, had long conversations with both Susan and Dave. I meditated in the afternoon. Hope tomorrow is a better day.

One aspect of depression is that it can manifest itself in such a way that the effects are physically felt. When you think about it, lack of sleep causes us to toss and turn all night and this can result in muscle aches or neck pain. In my case, couple that with not being able to eat due to severe anxiety and stomach acid multiplies, causing extreme discomfort. Bowels are affected by all of this as well. Headaches are often the result of lack of sleep, so there you go...stomach cancer, colon cancer, brain tumor. In 2000, I was convinced I had each of them.

Until the likelihood of having each affliction was individually ruled out, I experienced enormous anxiety. I even worried about my heart. I had every test available to man (or woman)...stress tests, blood work, EKG and a colonoscopy were but a few... and although the tests indicated that there was nothing wrong with me, I was still convinced that there was. Each time a fear was eliminated, it was replaced by two or three more. If my heart was healthy, maybe it was my lungs. That's it, lung cancer. The fears were never about minor medical problems, it was always the worst imaginable ones. I obsessed about it to the point of not being able to sleep... and then...I was suddenly thrown into the abyss.

FALLING FAST

The plunge was more rapid and of greater depths than ever before. It didn't take me long to know that this was clearly the worst episode ever, and, because of the dreadful symptoms and the sheer panic, I came close to doing the final deed. But death was not to come that easily.

My brothers and sisters had been calling daily, sometimes twice a day, because they now realized the seriousness of my condition. Their calls provided reminders that they were concerned and loved me, but the calls did very little to appease my pain. My obsessive thoughts of suicide continued and one morning, when these thoughts were particularly strong, the telephone rang.

SNAPSHOT
Oxford, Mississippi Late May 2000

Fran must detect the magnitude of my despair. I have said nothing more than "Hello," but the sound of a depressed person's voice can be telling. There is lifelessness, an emptiness that is immediately discernible. I know that she senses this. I tell her how awful I am feeling and she begins talking, setting up a wonderful analogy that results in providing me just enough hope.

"It's understandable, Ann," Fran says. "You are in the middle of a rain storm and the rain is pounding down. The wipers are at full speed, but they do nothing. You are not able to see beyond the storm, but the sun is on the other side and it will shine again. Remember how it was other times? Remember how you have managed to last out the storm? You think it's not possible and that the storm will last forever, but it won't. The sun is beyond."

The desperation in her voice is obvious, and I realize that she knows how despondent I am. I tell her that I know that what she is telling me is true, but knowing it and being able to wait out the horrific storm are two entirely different entities to this illness.

But, that day I decide to dismiss the thoughts of suicide.

ANGELS

As has been true so many, many times throughout my depressions, something would happen at *just* the right time that would result in my questioning my resolve to take my own life. It might be Gary walking in the door, or an unexpected call from a relative or friend, or a hug from Susan or Dave. It's as if people who love me take turns "waiting in the wings" and make themselves available to me when I most need them. I have a wonderful, loving family, both on my side and Gary's. Their support extends beyond me and they give much of their loving and caring to Gary as well. I count my blessings often, and it is because of them that I think hard about the decisions I make or choose not to make.

It is because I have so many reasons to endure the darkness that I can't help but wonder if many people who do not have such strong familial attachments do end up killing themselves. Believe me, waiting it out would not be my choice if I were alone. I would have much preferred to put an end to my agony, but I knew that I had many others to consider. But I also know that all of us are important to others. Those who don't have, or get along with, family may be close to colleagues, neighbors or friends; and, these people would be devastated if suicide was committed. Each of us is beholden to others, and has a responsibility to carefully consider the horror she/he would leave behind.

On the other hand, thousands of people much like myself, with strong family support, aren't able to wait to see the sun on the other side, as Fran had so aptly described it. What separates them from me? How is it possible to be strong enough not to do something that will erase my pain when I am so terribly weak? What is it that distinguishes those of us who are able to wait from others who are not?

I don't think there is one, or even a few, answers to why I managed to live. At times it was not having enough medication on hand or perhaps I would read in a book about suicide's effects on those left behind. At other times it may have been listening to a song on the radio that I loved which resulted in lifting my mood.

For others, it may be an array of other reasons. Many people become paralyzed with their depression. It's not possible to think through a plan, let alone complete it, if you are not able to function at all. Some sleep for days on end, thus providing a welcome escape from depression's grip. I was unable to.

I am convinced, however, that having a loving family that is physically there, people who are aware of your pain and are always holding you up, is a very critical factor in deciding to stay or just check out. At least it was for me. And, I think that mentioning the word *suicide* often makes the message others want to convey much more powerful than if it were just talked around. If you are concerned about someone, talk to him or her candidly about suicide. Use the word.

I CAN'T DO THIS ALONE

In the midst of all this—my not being able to eat, sleep or function—Gary left for a three-day conference. He wasn't gone more than a day when I realized I couldn't be alone because of the excruciating pain I was suffering. And I didn't know what to expect. When would I be able to sleep, stop losing weight, think clearly? This unpredictability added to my fears. And, like all of the other episodes, each minute seemed eternal.

"Gary, it's Ann. You've got to come home," I stammered over the phone.

"What's the matter?"

"I can't breathe, I am so afraid..."

He took the first plane he was able to book a day later and arrived home around midnight. I was in a fetal position on the living room couch, too depressed to cry or talk.

I knew that I was incapable of taking care of myself and I just wanted him there. I was more distressed than I had ever been. I was anxiety-ridden. I was panic-stricken. I was unable to be still because even when my body wasn't moving, my mind moved at a high-speed pace. Fears, doubts and regrets were consuming me...magnifying and growing larger by the second, I wanted to scream, but, of course, I was not able to. I had no strength to do anything. All I wanted to do was to die.

I was so disoriented that I was not able to keep track of the amount of medication I took each day. I had no system that would indicate whether or not I had taken my prescribed pills because I had no ability to think anything through. Have I taken my medicine? Maybe I haven't. Should I take it? Would it hurt if I have already taken it and I take more? Who the hell knows?

"Help me, please help me know what to do," I pleaded to no one in particular.

On consecutive days, I thought that I might have accidentally taken double doses. You see, at times I very much want to live and would panic when I think that I might not. One of the ironies of this illness...

Before Gary had returned, I even called a medication help center in Memphis and somehow managed to explain what had happened. The first day, the man on the other end of the line told me that it would be alright, but the second day he asked if I was alone. Looking at the call record he was aware that I had done the same thing the day before. I assured him that I was not suicidal, just confused.

Once Gary was back, he helped me establish a method of taking my daily dosage that would ensure that I knew whether or not I had taken the pills. Even then, it was difficult to think things through. The thing that worked best for me was to write down each time I took medication. Writing the specific pills, amounts and the time and date gave me something concrete as evidence of whether or not I had taken what I was supposed to take. The pad and pencil sat by the sink in the guest bathroom, near the pills.

DEJA VU...WITH SOME VARIATIONS

Here I was again...in a place where I had not been for fifteen years. Sure, I had experienced bouts of depression since that time, some were even severe, but they were short-lived and they were bearable. I had changed medications now and then...and there had been times when I so lacked self-confidence that I had to talk myself through each step of each day. Crashing like this? I thought it was all behind me.

My symptoms now bore resemblance to my severe fall in 1985. Once again unbearable. There was the anxiety, the insomnia and the panic. The hating to live and wanting to die feelings, constant this time...and much stronger than ever before. And now I had new symptoms. I was severely paranoid about whether we would be able to sell our Oxford home before we moved back. What if we had two mortgages at the same time? How could we manage?

Gary repeatedly had to remind me that all of that had not yet happened—and wasn't going to—but this made no difference to me. I worried about it all the time. I obsessed to the point of not being able to sleep. All the possibilities dominated my mind...what if, what if, what if? It was like I couldn't live in the present...my mind was only able to concentrate on what might happen in the future, and all that might happen was sure to be bad.

I had had enough. Once again I felt so terribly defeated. I knew from experience what it would take to get through it, and now I questioned whether I would be able to. One day I decided that I could not.

RATIONALIZATION

Maybe it was because my kids were grown. Maybe it was because I felt that Gary, Susan and Dave would be able to understand my escaping the intolerable place in which I existed. After all, they saw what it was doing to me. This was the first really good look at how I live with depression that Susan and Dave had seen. Now that they were adults they took serious notice. Surely they would fully grasp the reason behind what I so wanted to do. Wouldn't knowing that I was no longer suffering make my absence easier?

I rationalized my way into believing that suicide would be the best thing for all of us. I just could not again face the long uphill struggle that I knew was ahead. Or maybe it was because I was just too tired to continue...so very tired...so I decided to do the only thing I was able to do about it. I decided to take my life.

THE DECISION

There. I had done it...I had managed to make a decision at a time when I had not been able to make decisions. I hadn't been able to decide whether to walk around or lie down, whether to try to read or just sit on the deck, but I had no trouble making this decision. I was extremely relieved, knowing that the intense pain would be gone. It felt good making a decision. It felt good to make *this particular* decision.

Now that this was what I was going to do, I gathered every pill in the house, went into the guest bathroom and sat on the floor. Then I thought, shouldn't there be some sort of closure for Gary? He knew how terrible all of this was for me. But I certainly couldn't call him and say goodbye. The university was just minutes away so he could be home before I would be able to complete my plan. I could write him a letter, but I thought that it would be best if I wrote to someone else, someone who would let him know that this was something that I couldn't help doing. I knew that he would understand, but I wanted someone to be responsible for taking care of him.

Talk about ironic. I hadn't been able to care for myself for the past two months, let alone Gary, but I wanted someone to take over the job I wasn't doing.

So I wrote a letter to my brother, Ray. I told him that I could not endure any longer what I had somehow managed to endure all these years. I told him to take care of Gary. I signed it, took it out to our mailbox on the road in front of the house, and put up the red flag. Then I went back inside, intent on completing my plan.

What kind of a letter was that? Nothing about my kids or my grandkids, no note to Gary, just two sentences to the one sibling who has great difficulty dealing with emotional issues. And I expected *him* to be the strong one. This was certainly proof that I was not thinking clearly at all.

Back on the bathroom floor I really tried to put those pills in my mouth. I really, really wanted to, but it was as if a magnetic force would not allow my arm to move to my mouth. My mind desperately wanted only one thing, but my body simply would not allow it. It was eerie. So I sat there for what seemed like a long time, but was probably not long at all. When I came to the realization that what I wanted to do was not possible, I remembered the letter. Racing out the door (first time I had moved that quickly in over two months time!), I saw that the red flag was still up. I took the letter out of the box, brought it into the house and tore it up.

For years, the only person I ever told about this was Dr. Jon Bell, the Denver psychiatrist I had only spoken to long distance from Oxford. I would meet Dr. Bell a few weeks later and it would be during one of our sessions that I would tell him about the letter. I didn't have to tell Gary about my attempted suicide then because it wasn't going to happen (and then he would have known I'd planned to break my promise to him). I had to somehow go on. I resigned myself to this fact.

THE CONFESSION

Gary never learned about the letter until I started writing this book. My writing mentor, Dr. Judith Briles, suggested that I leave nothing out of my story in the telling. Knowing that this episode was certainly a major part of my memoir, I knew that I had to finally tell him.

It was early in 2006. We sat in the living room one evening, sharing our day with one another over a glass of wine. It felt like a good time to tell him about the letter that was never mailed, so I did. His eyes filled up, he looked at me and nodded, an indication that he was not surprised. He, more than anyone else, knew all too well how difficult living had been for me during those dark days. We laughed about the chosen recipient of my letter, however, because everyone in the family is aware of Ray's inability to handle anything unpleasant or confrontational. Gary confirmed my appraisal of this situation that this was a definite indication of my irrationality at that time.

CHAPTER 12:
The Trip from Hell

SNAPSHOT
Oxford, Mississippi A week later...

I hate decisions, particularly this one. Nothing is ever black and white...
two sides, weighing all options...it's exhausting, especially now.

It's hard enough to be weak, panicked and scared, let alone attempt to
think. There is no way that I could have done this.

This is one of those rare occasions that Gary made the decision without my
input. My input? Laughable!

But from the fateful day I tore up that letter, my condition continued to deteriorate. Gary and I talked about where I should be. Should I remain in Oxford, where I would be able to be with him, or should I return to Colorado, where I could be with our children, grandchildren and family?

I consulted on the phone with a good friend of Ray and Fran. Mary Chapman was a nurse practitioner whose specialization was counseling. I had known Mary and her husband, Steve, for years. Mary is one of those therapists who has never personally experienced depression but who understands it very well. She was a tremendous help in getting me through the days' decisions and I would call her often.

Mary and I discussed both sides of the issue at hand. Should I stay in Mississippi for the second year or return to Denver? She guided me through the pros and cons—a new list! — and told me that, ultimately, I would have to make the decision.

Gary and I continued to discuss this at length. It was too soon to see if the new medication would prove to be effective, so I was still severely depressed. It was clear that he was getting nothing done having to deal with me where I was. If I were to stay, we would be together, but, I rationalized, it was essential that I gain a bit of independence, at least for part of each day. Since we had no local therapists to ask, Gary contacted our real estate agent, Cherie Mathews, asking her for a recommendation for a therapist.

Cherie was the first person outside the university that we had met in Oxford. She had become a good friend over the past year. Small towns have a way of providing that to people who make the town their own. Gary felt comfortable calling her. Cherie suggested a hospital in Memphis that was known for working with mental health issues. Oxford was not known for its expertise in psychiatry. I had tried a psychologist a couple of times who, while certainly sympathetic, had not seemed to fully grasp the depth of my despair.

So, more plusses and minuses—if I were to remain with Gary there would be two people dealing with me...Gary and some unknown therapist. We would have to travel over an hour to Memphis several times a week and, because I was not capable of doing so, he would have to drive me there. In Colorado I would have many caretakers, an excellent psychiatrist and, most important, my children and my grandson. But there would be no Gary. Almost everything about going back to Denver appealed to me. I missed my children, my sisters and brothers and Denver in general. But having all of that and not having my husband with me was a huge negative.

So here we were again, going back and forth. Agonizing over it, I found myself talking to Mary Chapman a couple of times each day, and talking to Gary about it several times a day.

Then—I vividly remember this—it was a Tuesday evening in mid-July when Gary told me that he had made the decision that I should go back to Denver.

"I think it's best that you live with Ray and Fran rather than stay here," he told me. They were insisting they had room for me and I was welcome. "You're not capable of making a decision, so I'm making it for us. We will be leaving first thing Saturday morning, so get your things packed and we'll drive out."

No small task. Getting my things together was going to be difficult since concentration and planning are not in the vocabulary of someone in my state. More decisions. What and how much should I take...winter clothes, summer clothes? How long will I be there? In the end, I just piled nearly everything I regularly wore into the car. Nothing was organized, properly packed or thought out. The back seat of our car matched my chaotic life at that time.

I knew that Gary was right. I should be in Denver, and I felt relief that the decision was made. At that point, I would have been just as happy (had I been able to experience happiness at that time) if he had decided that I would be staying with him. I was just grateful to have it settled.

From the beginning, I had been adamant that Gary complete his commitment at the University of Mississippi. He understood the reason behind the final decision for me to return to Denver alone, as did both Susan and Dave. But I know that no one else understood it. Why would Gary stay there when I was so sick? How could a job be more important than the health of his wife? These were questions that I am sure many people asked one another.

GUILT...A HUGE PART OF MY DEPRESSION

The guilt! To understand, you'd have to be inside my head. Try to follow my thinking. It was because of me that we had returned to Pennsylvania in 1985 and then returned to Colorado the following summer. It was because of me that both Susan and Dave had spent college and high school years at three different schools. My family had given up a lot, running back and forth across the country. So I rationalized, remembering the guilt that was sure to return once I felt better. The guilt I had lived with was almost unbearable knowing that my illness had been such a disruption to their lives. How could I do this again? How would I be able to live with the guilt?

When in the midst of the nightmare that depression creates, I just wanted to feel better (I was unable to even feel any guilt at the time), and I believed that I would feel better somewhere else. This had happened on numerous occasions in the past, hadn't it? It would *have* to be better somewhere else because it would not be possible for it to be any worse.

Was I being selfish? Couldn't I see the damage that I created to the lives of my husband and children?

In the middle of it, these "selfish" moves seemed only to be self-preservation. But once they were made, I would then obsess about them—they were my "mistakes" once again. I watched everyone struggle to adjust and, inside, I just died. I was so very remorseful. And, even though I thought it was not possible to go further downward into depression, I knew living with the guilt I'd inflicted the last time had been so unbearable, I didn't want to create a situation where it would happen once again. This is why I desperately wanted Gary to stay through the commitment he had made. All those relatives and friends around me could never take his place, but I knew that he had to stay. He knew it also, and this, to us, was all that was important.

We could not control the way others saw the situation, the lack of respect I know that some of them harbored for Gary, but we knew that it was the only decision we could make. My mental health *had* to be our primary concern.

GARY: "Our move to Mississippi in the summer of 1999 was a mistake, we both see that now. I tried as I had so many times before to help her but I was totally ineffective. We talked and talked and talked. Neither the help coming from several doctors nor from me was making a difference.

"I had what was perhaps my most exciting and rewarding job—and Ann had nothing. She was in really bad shape emotionally and getting worse day by day. By this time several members of our family knew of Ann's new bout with depression. They were very concerned and some suggested that I should simply quit my job and immediately move back to Colorado. Both Ann and I knew that our situation was more complicated than that and that some who advocated an immediate resignation and move missed this complexity. Ann and I knew we faced a real Catch-22. Ann's depression was consuming her and a drastic change of some kind was immediately needed. At the same time, if I abruptly resigned, she would feel tremendous guilt and most likely be further depressed because of it.

"Faced with this, I made the unilateral decision that I was moving Ann back to Denver where she would have the safety net of children, grandchildren, siblings and friends. Aside from our strong marriage, this safety net had always been our greatest asset and we needed it now more than ever. I would stay on in Mississippi and finish out my year.

"For the year ahead, I would travel back and forth between Mississippi and Colorado as often as possible to be with Ann. Day in and day out the plan was to talk on the phone and in this way stay in continuous contact.

"The next day we loaded our car with many of Ann's clothes and we headed for Denver. It was a necessary but dreadful trip. Neither of us knew how all this would work out. What I expected would be two days of talking turned out to be just the opposite. I was afraid of what lay ahead and Ann was simply numb. We drove all that time with scarcely a word spoken. I was sure, however that had we stayed the course in Mississippi I just may have lost Ann. Relocating Ann in the way that we did was a chance worth taking.

"As it turned out, Ann lived with Ray, Fran and their kids for the better part of a year. Ray and Fran were just great, making Ann feel really at home and more a part of their family than ever before. As planned, we talked (and cried) every day. And when I could, I either drove or flew out to be with Ann for a few days.

"Being back among familiar places and having the family at hand was just what Ann needed and in time she got better and better. I never felt, however, that our marriage was ever in jeopardy. All told, we simply did what we had to do and by all accounts, the year apart was successful. Ann was pretty much back to normal and we were united again."

SNAPSHOT
Oxford, Mississippi April 2000

Depression is hell, so whether I am in Mississippi or Colorado, I still am in hell. It is one and the same. It doesn't make a bit of difference where I am, or knowing that others deeply care. Hell exists inside my mind and I am here to stay until I am released from depression's grip.

THE TRIP FROM AND TO HELL

The trip to Denver was simply dreadful. I was in such a state that I was unable to talk, read or even listen to the radio. It was a very long trip, particularly for Gary. I must have made him very worried. He told me later that en route to Colorado he thought that I had tried to swallow medication because I was in the motel bathroom longer than usual. He even had come into the room to make sure that that was not happening. I don't remember much about the trip, only that we didn't talk much.

There was a stranger in the car those two days, someone who was unrecognizable to the two of us. She thwarted our usual driving routine, insisted on selfishly having her way and...we hated her for it. Anyone who knows me knows that conversation is not something I lack. I am outgoing and verbal, so it was obvious to both of us that I was not even in the car. It was the Other Ann who was accompanying him on this Trip From and To Hell. And one hell of a trip it was!

* * *

Arriving in Denver, Ray and Fran had the guesthouse ready for me. They insisted I eat and be with the family during the day and early evenings. The nephews at home knew nothing about my depression. Nick, Alex and Matt had been told that I was homesick for the rest of the family, so I would be staying with them since our Denver house was being rented. Their older two children were aware of my depression, but I am certain that they did not know of its severity. Jennifer had graduated from the University of Missouri and was working as a television newscaster in Great Falls, Montana, and Mike was completing his senior year at the University of Kansas.

Even though everyone was considerate and loving, the rest of the summer was dreadful. Instead of feeling better having left Mississippi, severe anxiety had accompanied me to Colorado and I remember crying through every phone conversation Gary and I had. I saw Susan and Dave nearly every day and although my grandson Max, now two years old, was a diversion, I remained dead inside.

* * *

I had my first appointment with Dr. Jon Bell, my Denver psychiatrist, soon after we arrived. I had talked with him by phone several times when I was still in Mississippi. Now I would get help. Gary and I knew that it would be important that he go with me to Dr. Bell's office. When you are depressed, memory is not even a memory, so I could not be expected to fully comprehend the therapy session. I wanted him to go along so that we could both be a part of this latest round of therapy.

CHAPTER 13:
Hope

SNAPSHOT
Denver, Colorado May 2000

Gary and I anxiously await our appointment with Dr. Bell. I feel confident that he can help me since his expertise is antidepressant medication.

I'm not nervous…I value therapy, and know that it is crucial to my recovery.

Dr. Bell, thin and reserved, introduces himself and thus begins a professional relationship that still continues.

I begin to explain all that is happening to me. My symptoms would fill a textbook…severe anxiety, insomnia, weight loss…but I am particularly frightened by one particular symptom.

"I can't feel," I tell him.

It was during this first session that Gary fully grasped the depths of my despair. I had never been able to vocalize fully all of the things with which I am coping. I proceeded to try and tell Dr. Bell that I felt incredibly empty.

I told him that, just the day before, Max had put his little arms around my neck and said, "I love you, Grammy." But when he did this, nothing happened inside. It was as if a stranger with whom I had no emotional ties was talking to me. This was a frightening realization. I remember incredulously telling myself, "I… feel… nothing."

> As I told Dr. Bell this, I caught a sideways glimpse of Gary and saw terror written on his face.

I knew that my depression was far, far worse than it had ever been because I had never before experienced complete lack of feeling. All those years my children were growing up, their presence had always made me feel better. Why wasn't this happening with Max, the child whose birth we had so long awaited? I was so empty, but at least I did recognize this meant that I needed help more than I had ever needed it before. And needing and wanting help meant I would find Ann again.

SNAPSHOT
Denver, Colorado June 2000

Sitting on the small couch in Susan's Steele Street home, I am in deep despair. Susan is next to me. As she puts her arm around me, she says, "Mom, promise me that you will never commit suicide."

Feeling nothing, I flatly respond, "I promise."

That was all that was said, but that was the first time that anyone had ever used the word in association with my depression.

"How did he or she die?" you might ask someone upon learning of a recent death.

"He committed suicide" is often the response. Suicide. What an appalling word. I inwardly cringe when I hear it. I think that I always have...even when I was much younger, many years before depression became a part of my life. To me, it creates a neon sign in my mind that screams FINAL... DESPAIR... SEVERE

UNHAPPINESS... WEAKNESS... GRIEF OF THOSE LEFT BEHIND... and, for a brief moment or two, *I* grieve for all that that person left behind as well as for those who knew and loved him or her.

If it were someone I knew well, my thoughts would linger. At one time I spent much time thinking about all the "if onlys"...if only someone had known the extent of the problem, if only the person had sought help...and I believed that maybe, just maybe the suicide could have been prevented. I no longer believe that, so "don't dwell" and "if only" are no longer a part of my thinking when a suicide is the result of deep despair. This bears repeating: I do think that family and friends can *delay* this act, but they can't physically *prevent* it. The most you can hope for is that suicidal urges are delayed long enough for medication to take effect. And if that person isn't taking medication, it becomes much more difficult.

I have thought about suicide often. I have seen that word in my mind thousands of times, enticing me towards it because beyond that word is peace, a place where I would be free of pain.

Its temptation has pulled like a siren, beckoning. "Come here," it whispers. "This is where you will find pure happiness, happiness unlike any you have ever known."

It has not been easy pulling away from this force because the weakness this illness creates makes me so vulnerable. How can I have strength to reject this choice? How can I find the strength to complete it? Why haven't I given in?

It is the illness itself that has come to my rescue time and time again. The indecision and inability to concentrate that is so prevalent works in my favor at these times. I am incapable of thinking through a plan, incapable of finding an appropriate time or place. I am incapable of anything other than breathing...so, other than the plan I desperately wanted to complete in Oxford, there have been hundreds of times that I have gotten no further than the thoughts. The thoughts comfort me.

Once again, even if I *could* complete a plan, I have just promised to Susan that I wouldn't. I didn't want to promise, but I did. I have to keep my promises... children know that and this is my adult child. Our roles are reversed and she is making me promise something that I don't want to agree to; but, because she is the strong one, I listen to her. And I hate myself for doing it.

A SON'S DESPERATE PLEA

One afternoon, while visiting with Susan and lying on Susan and John's bed because I could no longer tolerate being around people, Dave appeared at the door. I was in anguish, and, once again, I was wondering if I would be able to get through it. All of this was apparent to my son.

He sat down on the bed and asked me how I felt. He already knew the answer. I told him I just wanted to be alone for a while, but that I knew I would feel better soon. Of course, I didn't know that. I never know whether or not I will feel better. I wasn't fooling either one of us. Words, just words.

As he started to leave, Dave turned around at the door.

"Mom," he said. "I just want you to know that just because I am grown up doesn't mean I don't need a mom."

His words cut deeply. I knew what he was telling me. I needed to be reminded of this. Because so much of my rationalization (and I rationalized plenty) was based on the fact that both Susan and Dave were now grown, I needed to be reminded that we never really grow up. We always need our mom.

My mother had died quite suddenly in 1988, the year I turned forty-six. We were living in Pueblo at that time, having moved there just a year and a half earlier. Mom had loved the fact that we had "come home," and we loved being so close to her once again. We enjoyed our spur of the moment dinner invitations, Christmas shopping with one another, and being so close you could just drop by the house. Our return to Pueblo had, in many ways, been a gift to both of us.

When she died, I missed her terribly. I still do. I miss the phone calls I regularly received...the second one minutes after we would hang up because she "forgot" to tell me something.

Thinking about how much I missed my mom, I knew that I, too, would be missed. Just as I believed I still needed a mom, my two children would feel the same.

"I know, Dave," I answered.

"I want you to be there when I get married in October. I want you to be there when I have children someday. I still need you," he continued.

"I want that too, Dave," I responded. "Thanks."

He left. The doorway was empty, and I had once again made a promise to one of my children.

I felt disappointment because I knew that as much as I wanted to alleviate this pain, I could no longer think of suicide as an option. I had promised...and promises must be kept.

As I struggled to recover from this depression, I often thought about both of these incidences. I thought about the desperation and the pleading in their voices. I thought about how hard I would have to work in order for them to still have their mom...and I never forgot the two promises I had made.

HOPE...COULD THERE BE?

When I had finished trying to explain what had been occurring to me inside, Dr. Bell looked me straight in the eyes and said, " I can tell you this, you *will* get better."

I grabbed onto the only piece of hope I had had for the past two months. I knew that I *had* to get better. I had a second grandchild arriving any day and Dave and Kelly were to be married in the fall. I couldn't be responsible for destroying their happiness, not only once again but also forever. I told myself that I had to get better. Dr. Bell had just said that I would and now I, too, believed that it was possible. I still felt empty, but at least the words were absorbed.

Everyone was very concerned about my mental health, and indications of this reinforced my importance to them. I knew that those who loved and cared for me were there to help in any way they could. I knew that this was a positive thing, and I was aware that I loved them all—but right now, it was an empty love.

MY COLORADO SUPPORT SYSTEM

Only my two children and Ray and Fran knew the extent of my condition, even though other family members were aware that I was depressed. Without all the details, it was not possible for any of them to grasp the scope of my struggle, but I knew that they cared just the same.

The emptiness continued, but activity around me certainly kept me busy. My brother and sister-in-law and their three children who still lived at home were absolutely wonderful to me. Ray and Fran always had words of encouragement, and provided comfort and lots of love. They never made me feel as if I were intruding.

Ray would walk onto his patio, calling up to my window. "Annie, are you up? It's a great day." Of course, to me it was anything but a great day. It was yet another long day with which I had to contend.

The boys were told that I left Mississippi because I missed my grandson and wanted to help my daughter with the expected arrival of another child. Like their mom and dad, my nephews accepted me as one of the family, introduced me to all their friends and asked me for help on homework when they needed it. I told them several years later that it was actually my health that had brought me to their house. Regardless of the reason, the opportunity for a deeper relationship with all of them was one of the bright sides of that extended time with the family.

We kept busy. Fran would take me with her when she picked up one of my nephews, I was included each time their family went out to dinner, and Dave, Susan, John and Max spent lots of time with me. We went to the swimming pool, the zoo and the playground. Fran would leave notes stuck to the coffee pot, written verification of her love and concern:

"Help yourself, and think about having another piece of that birthday cake."

"Want to go with me to yoga?"

These kindnesses did lift me a bit, giving me something to do that, in turn, made my long days go somewhat faster. But I wanted each day of being sociable to come to a close because then I could go over to the guesthouse and just be by myself. Gary, in the meantime, would call several times a day and, as I am certain he could correctly predict would happen, I cried as he reassured me that things would eventually be good. After all, we had a grandchild and were expecting another any day, and a daughter-in-law that would soon join our family, so it was important that I do what I could to share these blessed events. I should be glad that I was there, he said, that I could see everyone everyday rather than sit alone in the house in Mississippi. I was glad, but glad had a very different meaning at this time of my life.

ROLE REVERSALS

That summer, when Gary was in Mississippi and before I moved to Ray and Fran's house, my children became my parents. They called often to check on me and I spent quite a bit of time with Susan, John and Max. Dave was still living in Pueblo and would move to Denver shortly before the October wedding when he and Kelly would be married.

I stayed at Susan and John's so that I could be there when our new grandchild arrived. Some help I was! Fluctuating moods, crying spells and telephone conversations with Gary much of each day was not the way to lessen Susan's work...in fact, it created much more.

The house on Steele Street was small, a bungalow amidst newly constructed upscale condominiums that had replaced previous small bungalows. A makeshift bed in the basement family room consisted of a single-sized mattress atop box springs. I would hear small steps on the basement stairs each morning, followed by a tiny face peeking down at me.

"Are you getting up? Want some pancakes, Grammy?" Max would say.

Although getting out of bed is terribly difficult when depression is around, this was not true on these mornings. What an enticement...my grandson smiling as he continued to totter down the remaining steps. He'd cuddle with me in bed, sometimes clutching a book for the two of us to read together.

My son-in-law and I developed an evening routine. He would bake large chocolate chip cookies with a huge scoop of vanilla ice cream on top and serve them to Susan and me after Max had been put to bed. I experienced no guilt as I consumed those calories. I desperately needed to gain the weight that depression had stripped from my body, so I eagerly complied.

Going places with Susan and Max was a real diversion...sometimes my mood lifted, other times it did not. One particular day Susan and I decided to take Max to the zoo. I wasn't doing well, but agreed to accompany them. Susan helped me into the car, went around to the other side and carefully buckled Max into his car seat. Then she hoisted her very pregnant self into the Pathfinder and sighed as she gave me a slight smile.

"It's not easy getting a toddler, a depressed mom and me off for the day." Here she was, nine months pregnant, doing the best she could. We both had a good laugh because it was true. I was no help at all; if anything, I was a thorn to all that we did together.

On June 27, our precious Anna Elizabeth arrived close to the time of day I was born fifty-eight years earlier. Both Gary and I witnessed her birth and cried as we welcomed her into our world. Susan, tears falling fast, exulted, "I'm so happy I have a girl," she cried. As I witnessed family and friends who soon crowded into her hospital room, I told God that I was thankful to be here, sharing this beautiful moment, rather than the alternative, which I know now would have lessened the joy for everyone else.

* * *

It's very strange that just when you think you have no strength at all, you somehow manage to have some when it's necessary. That summer, my Kochenberger sisters-in-law were hosting a bridal shower for Kelly. The shower was in Pueblo, a two-hour drive from Denver. It looked as if I would not be able to have the strength necessary to go to this event, even though I desperately wanted to. Every morning had been the same for the past three months...the dark, heavy feeling of dread was the very first thing that occurred to me before my eyes even opened.

Yet the day of the shower I awoke and felt happiness. It was as if God had given me a gift that would allow me to get through that day. Perhaps He had made the decision to spare me the guilt I would have endured had I not gone, the attention I would have drawn to myself and the explanations I would have had to provide. I went to the shower feeling extremely grateful, but I was very weak and my nerves were frayed. I had a hard time sitting still. But I made it.

It was during the latter part of August that I began to get better. I was keeping a record of my daily progress in my journal, rating my mood for a given day as my Denver doctor, Dr. Alan Feiger, had suggested nearly twenty years earlier. The number 3 dominates the pages beginning August 24, soon after which I recorded that top number on eleven consecutive days. Keeping that record was important because the bad days seem to be much longer while the good days fly by. If I would have a bad day and would look over my journal I would often be very surprised that I had had so many good days. You only remember the bad...

SUSAN: "I first realized you were having problems when I was in high school. I knew you were seeing a therapist and I would sometimes drop you off at Sandy's office. Dad would often tell me to go give you a hug or to tell you that I loved you, so I knew that you must have needed reassurance.

"My perception was that you were stable and functional, and you were. You talked about your bio- rhythms, often saying that they were low, and you also meditated daily. I must have known that you were depressed, but you always provided explanations for your sadness.

"My first experience seeing my mom seriously depressed was when we moved to Denver in 1984 and I was at a freshman DU. I remember coming home and she was sitting on the floor against the wall in her bedroom crying, with Kleenex all around her. She was missing Pennsylvania and couldn't cope with the new reality. Dad told me that she was seeing a therapist off and on. I was thrilled to be in Colorado and having a great time in school.

"Mom managed to function that year and work and laugh while enjoying family and relatives, but plans were already underway to return to State College, a desperate decision to hopefully help her recover. In the late spring of 1985, she flew out ahead of us to look for housing. Dad, Dave and I drove the van filled with furniture and the car in which our cat, Poco traveled.

"All along the three-day journey we were told that there was a call from mom each time we checked into a motel. Dad would return her call and listen to her admitting what a mistake it was to move back while begging dad to turn around and return to Denver.

"Going back to State College was hard. I was sad to leave Denver. Knowing that we might only be there a year, I made up my mind to study hard so that the time would go much faster. I didn't affiliate with my sorority or completely connect with the college life, but I had some good times that year. I felt okay about it.

"When my mom came out from Mississippi at the end of April in 2000, she was so despondent – the worst I had ever seen her. In May she was back and forth between Oxford and my house in Denver. I remember that she went to see Dr. Bell soon after coming to Denver. She was consistently down, although sometimes she would be good for a portion of the day, then bad again. Every time John came home from flying, he would signal me when mom wasn't looking, thumb up or down, to gauge how she was.

"I would try to encourage her to go for walks, but she was resistant. She lost a ton of weight. Dad was in Mississippi so mom called him a lot or he would call her. She kept asking me whether she should go back to Mississippi or stay in Denver. Decisions of any size were monumental for her, and she harbored a lot of guilt about not being able to stay in Mississippi.

"When my mom lived with us before Anna was born at the end of June, it was hard because the house was tiny and I was taking care of her as well as Max. She was frustrated and irritable and she worried about money; she hoarded money one day and spent money the next day, although never very much.

"Sometimes she was too high, laughing and talking too fast or acting irrational. Mom admitted to being suicidal and I knew she had enough prescription drugs to pull it off. The possibility would cross my mind, but I never really believed that she would go through with it. This was probably naive on my part.

" I made her promise me that she wouldn't commit suicide and she made that promise. Of course I realized that that was no guarantee that she wouldn't, but it reassured me a bit and I hoped that it would make her think harder about it.

"Just in case she was seriously considering suicide, I would purposely engage her in discussions about future milestones and life events that she would deny herself if she took her life. She completely understood what I was doing and she participated in these discussions, helping me brainstorm graduations, reunions and parties that we could anticipate one day.

"The most eminent event at that time was the birth of our second child, due just weeks away. Max, our first born, was 26 months when Mom stayed with us and he offered a great distraction. Mom and Max had a special connection.

"Nearly every night as she retreated downstairs to her bedroom, I would say "I'll send Max down in the morning to wake you up" knowing that she would never subject Max to the horror of discovering a non-responsive or deceased grandmother."

CHAPTER 14:
Home at Last

Serzone prescription was increased to 500mg. On the 12th of this month, then up again to 600 mg on the 25th. I am to take it twice daily, but with or without food? The Ambien I am taking for sleep is helpful to a degree, but does it help anxiety? Now that I had to stop the Xanax, how do I deal with this anxiety?

I think I was manic for three days. Questions to ask Dr. Bell:

1. How do you define mania?
2. How long should I give this Serzone before we discuss a medication change?

I am to call him in a week. It will be a very long week.

As I began to feel better, I saw Dr. Bell frequently. I was calling him most every day. The time between my call to him and his return call always seemed endless. In truth, he always returned calls promptly.

I was taking new medication and, as was always the case, this involved an adjustment period. Side effects are always possible and how well I would tolerate a new drug was something that only time would determine. In the meantime, I was having longer periods of time during each day when I felt better.

WHY DID IT HAPPEN?

In one of my sessions with Dr. Bell that summer I asked him why he thought I'd had this recurrence.

"Well, let's think about it, Ann," he answered slowly, "You lost your home, you left your job, your family, the familiar places you had frequented. You left your children in Colorado, the grandson you so cherish was no longer nearby and Susan was expecting the baby momentarily. You were planning a wedding long distance and now, because of your mental instability, you and Gary faced a year of separation! Wouldn't that be enough to cause severe depression?"

Well, when he put it that way! I could now see everything more clearly. Even someone with no history of depression would have had a difficult time adjusting. It was no wonder that I had been so vulnerable. I will never forget his description of my condition: I was *susceptible to instability*.

I think that sometimes we expect everyone's life to stop when we are not in the midst of it. This is naïve, to be sure, but, even though I knew that Susan and John wanted a sibling for Max, I didn't expect it to be so soon. I didn't anticipate the guilt I would feel knowing Susan could use my help in Colorado. Guilt is one thing on which I am an expert. I have perfected feeling guilty...it weighs heavily. There had been no way we could have predicted that I would feel so deprived by not being in Colorado that year, with all the activity I was missing.

Dave hadn't even met Kelly prior to our leaving Colorado, yet, just seven months later, our family was celebrating their engagement and upcoming marriage and we were eagerly awaiting our second grandchild's impending birth. Missing Max far, far more than I imagined was particularly painful, and this only worsened as the depression set in because emotions are felt more deeply during those times. Healthy people can cope with all of that, but I was not able to. I had forgotten that I am not an emotionally healthy person and that good times are merely remissions rather than forever.

YET ANOTHER DECISION

Since I had returned to Denver a year earlier than planned, Ray encouraged me to try to get a teaching position that year rather than wait until the following one. He felt that it would be good for me to be busy and gain confidence at the same time. I had reservations about it because, even on the new medication, while I felt good on some days, I was still depressed on others. I questioned whether I had the ability to do a good job.

After giving it much thought and discussing it with Gary, I decided to interview with my district and was granted a part-time 6th grade position at the middle school in the area. I had never taught at that level, but by being a big part of the lives of thirty-four nieces and nephews (not an exaggerated number) at that time, I comfortably connect with kids of that age. I would be part of a team, teaching with a woman who had been at the school for several years. Knowing that I would be able to have a certain amount of guidance was reassuring.

And the fact that I had a teammate who would mentor me and that my job would be part-time was a blessing. I could work half a week, and I would certainly welcome the help from a seasoned teacher. I was much more comfortable with my decision once I realized this.

After I started the job, some days I was actually happy, but there were many days when I felt trapped. Now I couldn't go back to see Gary at will because I had responsibilities. Flexibility was not an option. This was the same feeling of entrapment I'd had when we left State College and moved to Denver. My signing of the teaching contract resulted in dredging up those same dreadful emotions.

BLESSINGS, LIKE BAD LUCK, SOMETIMES COME IN THREES

Again, God seemed to be watching over me when I discovered that my teammate was a young woman named Michelle Ansley. I knew of Michelle's reputation and I had heard wonderful things about her teaching expertise. My respect for Michelle heightened as we discussed lesson plans each week. Very capable, with an amazing ability to connect with kids, Michelle was a tremendous role model for me. She explained that we would be splitting up the week. I would teach full days Monday and Tuesday and until noon each Wednesday. She would take the rest of the week. We both taught language arts and social studies, so we planned each week as a team.

She explained *everything* to me...the grading system, how she ran the classroom, her high expectations. I was able to observe her for two days before I began teaching on my own. She was "no nonsense" with kids and they rose to the occasion. I have tremendous respect for Michelle and consider myself very fortunate to have had the privilege of teaching with her.

The teaching was good for me because it provided a purpose. I loved teaching at that level and the subjects I taught were coincidentally my two favorites. I learned right along with the class since I had never been involved with middle school curricula. I was pleased that I was quickly able to adapt to this new level of teaching and confidently get back to business. I also had very good rapport with my students, some of whom I continue to correspond with via e-mail five years later.

Spending half the week away from the classroom was just what I needed at that time of my life. I would remain at school Wednesday afternoons, writing lesson plans and correcting papers in my office. I would often be the only person at home on Thursday and Friday since Fran taught as well and my three nephews were in school.

My flexible schedule also allowed me to be away from Denver for consecutive days. I went back to Mississippi on a few occasions, but I would more often go to Colorado Springs and stay with my sister Susan for several days. I always felt so comfortable with her; and if I had schoolwork that needed to be completed, I was able to do it at her home.

Yes, there were wonderful times during that year about which I will always have fond memories. I was able to spend much time with Max and, after the June 27 birth of our precious Anna, I was able to enjoy her as well.

My relationship with each of the three Baker nephews who lived at home deepened. Matt and I discussed his school days as I took him to and from practice, Alex told me all about his classes and Nick and I stayed up late editing his papers and talking about the family members whose deaths prevented him ever knowing them. It was, quite honestly, an opportunistic time for all of us to get to know one another on a much more profound level than we otherwise would have.

But the other times...when I was depressed? The time seemed endless.

READJUSTING... AGAIN

Gary and I were determined to keep our pledge to be together often. Our time apart made our time together special. Of course, there were small adjustments that we laugh about now. When I moved into the guesthouse at Ray's, I began using Gary's side of the bed because that was where the nightstand was placed. It was not possible for me to move it to the other side because the bed was against the wall. I adjusted to this rather quickly as I read each night before the light was turned off.

So, back in Oxford, since I had become accustomed to sleeping on the opposite side back in Denver, I found it difficult to sleep on my usual side. Arguing that that had always been his side of the bed, Gary reluctantly gave in after the first occasion.

Another adjustment concerned decision-making. As Christmas neared I told Gary that we would be spending Christmas Eve at my uncle's home because all of my brothers and sisters would be home that year. Given that we always spent Christmas Eve at his mother's house, he not only objected, but also was angry that I alone had made such a major decision. He reminded me that we had always discussed things in the past and said that he resented being blindsided.

After thinking about it for several minutes, I realized that he was right. I had become accustomed to having to consider only myself when plans were being made. I had unintentionally failed to consult him. This situation was reminiscent of the many times I was so depressed that he made all the decisions, something I resented him doing, once I was beginning to recover.

I LOVE THIS HOUSE

Once the school year ended, I spent a month in Mississippi before we packed up and headed back to Denver. It was wonderful to once again be in our house. There were many days when I would exhilarate in the fact that we were home, silently telling myself "I love this house." It's a very unsettling feeling to be without a home and I am so thankful to have been able to share Ray and Fran's home. The guesthouse "belonged" to me for that year but, although I felt more comfortable there as time went by, I desperately missed my own house.

We began to adjust (a most welcome adjustment this time) to being home and spent the summer trying to gain back what had been lost. Naturally, that was not possible. We had endured a very difficult year that had resulted in many changes within each of us, but these changes were good ones. Our respect for one another heightened even more, and we had a deeper appreciation for Susan and Dave and for our extended family.

Today, when I look back on that awful year, 2000, I am amazed that I was able to survive. Coming to Colorado without Gary was one of the most difficult things I have ever done. Traveling to Colorado Springs and Oxford so often, and living out of suitcases, was both a blessing and a curse for my shattered nerves.

But I did the best that I could do, knowing that it would eventually be over and that we would have a normal life once again.

I will never forget one evening in particular. Gary and I were back home, sitting on our deck, sipping wine and exulting in the fact that we had somehow survived the year...

"You know, Gary," I said, "it's hard to believe that the year is over. I know how terrible it was for you, and I want you to know how grateful I am to have you. But, even though it must have been a nightmare for you and I may have more periods of depression, I emphatically know that you would never leave me."

There was a long pause. Then he turned and looked at me and said, "You know...you really *are* crazy."

Part 3

COPING STRATEGIES

This section is truly the heart of Out of Focus…Again. In it are the many things I did to prevent myself from taking my life. I have used these strategies innumerable times to get through, not just the day or the hour, but through each minute of each hour of each day as I battled through the hell that this illness creates.

Reading Part III will enable you to incorporate "more" to combat the symptoms of depression in such a way that you will be able to eliminate the "less" from hopeless, thereby turning a negative word into a very positive one.

CHAPTER 15:
Whatever Works

I don't think that people with severe depression think about what will cure them because it's difficult to think beyond the moment. The moment is all you can manage. It's all about coping, and coping is as complex as the illness. Time management takes on new meaning. I felt that I could handle bits of time rather than think of a day in its entirety. It is simply overwhelming to imagine getting through all of those hours. For me, survival was all about all the little things along with the major strategies of therapy and medication that enabled me to continue.

Having a therapist skilled in all the nuances of depression is essential. Many therapists read a few articles and consider themselves knowledgeable, but people such as these are not what you want. It is vital that you have someone who specializes in mental health illnesses, therapy and medication. I discuss both medication and therapy in this section.

The most important thing I learned about coping is that it is ongoing. I learned not only what worked for me, but also how to be proactive in preventing a situation that might stimulate or worsen the depression.

MISERY HAS COMPANY

Did you know Abraham Lincoln endured years of depression? He once said that it is not whether you will get through it; you know that you will. What is not certain is whether you will be able to wait that long. His assessment is an accurate one. When coping, your inner resources are truly tested.

Depression does not discriminate. In addition to Lincoln, well-known people such as William Styron, Mike Wallace and Patty Duke are very familiar with its pain. Jane Pauley, Luci Arnez and Dick Cavett are a few others. Many of them have written about how it has affected their quality of life. I found such readings very beneficial and could identify with their experiences; I gained information and ideas from the reading. All of this gave me a huge sense of comfort because it was validation that I was not alone, I wasn't *"really* crazy"! And if I was, I was certainly in good company.

Along with reading about my illness, I exercised. The fact that I jogged routinely may have saved my life. Once I got out and started running, I somehow was able to elevate my mood a little. The problem was getting going. It took inner strength and determination just to get dressed and out the door. While I knew that I would feel much better after I ran, I was never sure I had either the mental strength to make the decision to accomplish it or the physical strength to actually put one foot in front of the other. Depression saps ambition.

I know all the various ways to cope differs for each person. The running that I discovered was so effective for me does not necessarily work for everyone. I have also come to realize that what works for me at a given time may not be effective at another time. Medication and therapy are helpful—I would call them lifelines—for most people, but beyond these two things, it's simply whatever works.

Most of us take routine and predictability for granted. We go to bed thinking about what we will do the following day, never stopping to consider that we may or may not be able to accomplish the goals we set. We wake up, get dressed, get the kids off to school, then make beds and do dishes...all on automatic mode. We contend with traffic, with time management and with stress and all of it is smooth and natural. But when one is depressed, none of it happens the way it's supposed to.

To get anything done, I implemented what I call "coping strategies" or "coping procedures." These were little tricks or techniques—some not so little, as you will see—that I would put into place because they made my day easier. Each of them was important, some more than others; some were immediate, while others were ongoing. A few took long periods of time to reach or complete, but all of them were vital to my ability to survive each minute of each and every day.

CHAPTER 16:
Religion and Prayer

I awoke remembering a strange dream. I dreamed that I was holding a religious shroud, somewhat like a tapestry. As I held it in front of my chest, it began to glow, radiating a light of intense brilliance.

As the light permeated my entire body, I felt tremendous warmth and, as this warmth was experienced, I felt comfort and love of such intensity I have never before experienced. When I woke up I knew that I was loved...and I knew it was God who was sending me reassurance.

This was the first of many religious visualizations that would occur during that time, the year we moved from Denver back to State College. As I recalled this particular dream I would feel unbelievable inner peace and a remarkable amount of encouragement. It gave me strength when I had none.

I have accepted these visions as valid. I know what I saw and felt and never questioned them. I was also aware that God's love and concern were specifically for me rather than for the inclusive concern of everyone.

My religion, first and foremost, has provided tremendous comfort. During times when I am experiencing the symptoms of depression I pray a lot. I pray at mass or go to church in the middle of the day; I pray at home or in the car. It is no exaggeration when I say that sometimes I pray almost the entire day. I ask God to please help me get through the day, to give me determination and strength.

Prayer provides reassurance. For me, it is somewhat like journal writing in that it allows thoughts to be spoken silently and, just as importantly, I need no one else to accomplish it. No appointments are necessary and it can be done anywhere, at any time. For these reasons, this is the coping device that has been most available. It's there anytime I need it. No matter what your religion or beliefs, if you are able to pray, you can find enormous comfort. And, if you have no religion meditation or just sitting amidst nature provides a calming effect.

FINDING MY WAY BACK

Throughout our marriage, Gary and I attended churches of many denominations. We were quite active in the Unitarian Fellowship for many years. I loved the church and looked forward to attending, but when depression first entered my life I returned to Catholicism. I had been raised in the Catholic Church. It's familiarity provided comfort and I felt it was where I belonged. Maybe I felt as if "God saw me grow up there," attending mass with my mother and Susan. And maybe some part of me believed that it would be easier for God to find me if I was in the place where he had always known me to be. Sounds silly, doesn't it, but I wasn't making much sense then anyway. I was doing whatever I could to just feel better and I felt most comfortable with the first religion I had known.

I have always felt valued by God and know that there is a higher power supporting me. Being Catholic enables me to pray, not only to God and Jesus, but to Mary as well.

My non-Catholic friends think that we put Mary on the same level as we do God and Jesus, but this is not true. We do, however, feel that she is pretty high up there, because she was chosen to be the mother of Jesus. We revere her, but do not put her on the same level as her Son and His father.

And then there are all the saints to whom one can pray. Many of the saints are prayed to because of their love of or concern for special causes, giving them the status of "patron saint." St. Francis loved birds and small animals, so people often place a statue of him in their garden. St. Theresa of Lisieux, a saint who is portrayed in statues all over the world, is one of our more popular saints. Many attribute this fact to her "ordinariness." She is known as the "Little Flower" and can often be seen holding a bouquet of roses, commemorating her promise to "let fall a shower of roses" and other favors after her death. She was declared co-patroness of France in 1947, sharing this esteemed honor with St. Joan of Arc.

I think every Catholic aligns him or herself with several saints to whom they pray for specific causes. I have always loved St. Theresa of Lisieux, probably because there is a church bearing her name in my hometown. Many believe that if you pray to St. Theresa and receive a rose, it is a sign that your wish will be granted. I have prayed to her often and, interestingly, *have* received roses. My prayers have usually been a plea for the abatement of my depression and roses give me much relief because I believe that she has, indeed, intervened.

Many Catholics honor St. Christopher, the Patron Saint of Travel. His medal can often be seen hanging from mirrors or on the dashboards of cars. St. Jude is our patron saint of "lost causes" so prayers to him ask for his intervention when people are critically ill or injured.

MIRACLES

Reading about and listening to people recount personal religious experiences has always intrigued me. While I believed that such things sounded implausible, I never completely discounted them. Who am I to question what other people emphatically say is true? Reading accounts of former "nonbelievers" whose religious occurrences caused them to completely change their way of thinking made me wonder if such events do, in fact, occur. I now know that they do.

That dream in which I had the visualization proved that God did love me. He knew of my despair and had sent me a message that this personal love was real. I had talked to Him tens of thousands of times throughout my life...in prayer and in conversation, but until now, He had never responded. Not that I ever needed verification. I knew that my prayers always reached Him and, after all, God's plenty busy! But that night He did respond.

Another religious experience occurred in 1986 during a time I was awake.

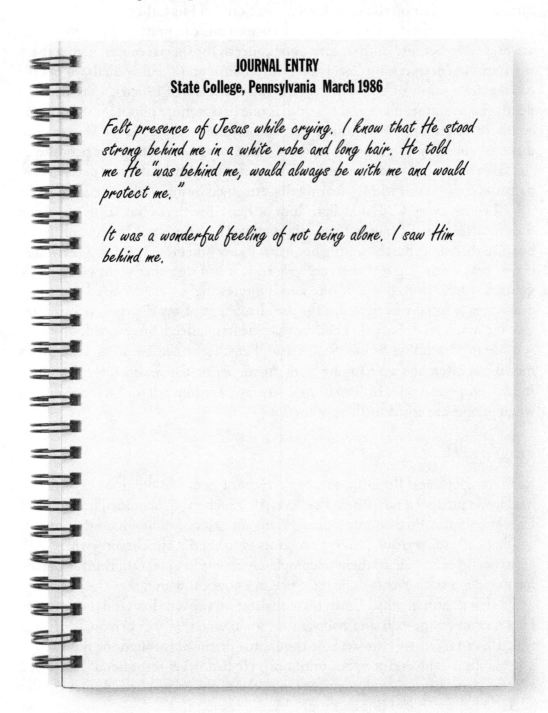

JOURNAL ENTRY
State College, Pennsylvania March 1986

Felt presence of Jesus while crying. I know that He stood strong behind me in a white robe and long hair. He told me He "was behind me, would always be with me and would protect me."

It was a wonderful feeling of not being alone. I saw Him behind me.

I never turned around to see if Christ was really there. It wasn't necessary because I knew that He was. This vision was from above, as if I were standing above the entire scene. I saw myself on the floor and Jesus behind me. The message He sent was not spoken. I heard no words, but a message was nonetheless received. I have never questioned the authenticity of this vision.

I did mention it to Sandy at my following therapy session and he remarked, "Oh, you had an out of body experience." It was then that I realized that was exactly what had happened.

Jane Koot had been a good friend since 1970, the first year we moved to State College. She knew that I had been depressed both in Denver and upon returning to town in 1985. She had been attending a Catholic prayer group on the Penn State Campus, and suggested that I might want to go along. It was during one of the weekly prayer group meetings that a third apparition occurred in the spring of 1986.

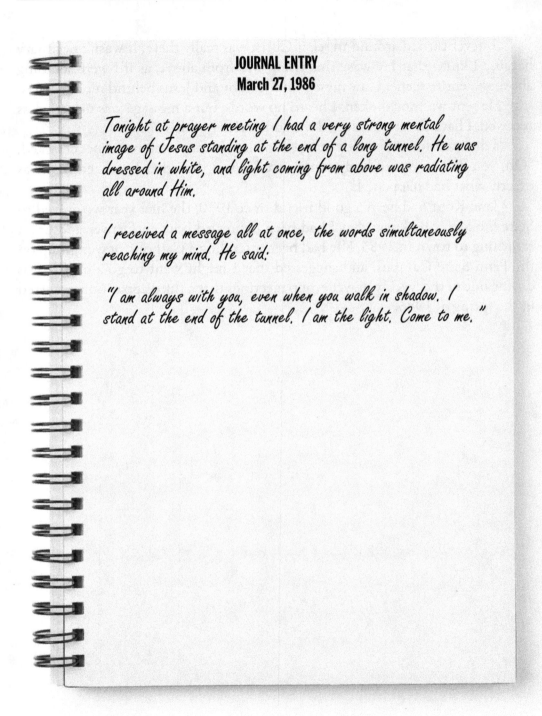

JOURNAL ENTRY
March 27, 1986

Tonight at prayer meeting I had a very strong mental image of Jesus standing at the end of a long tunnel. He was dressed in white, and light coming from above was radiating all around Him.

I received a message all at once, the words simultaneously reaching my mind. He said:

"I am always with you, even when you walk in shadow. I stand at the end of the tunnel. I am the light. Come to me."

I remember that these words were so emphatic. Driving home I realized that I had received a prophecy through which Jesus was telling me to stay close to him. Fearful that I would forget the words before I wrote them down, I drove home quickly so that I could record them in my journal. But I never forgot them. This was the most profound religious experience that I have had and, even today, I can still feel the emotion those words evoked. It's like I am reliving this prophecy each time I recall it. That evening remains stored in my memory and in my heart.

The last significant religious encounter occurred sometime later, during the same spring of 1986 and came in the form of a vision. While at prayer group, I received a mental image of Christ in a doorway, arms reaching out toward many lambs that gathered around Him. Light was everywhere, and He was smiling lovingly as he extended His arms, gathering them with His hands. I later learned that lambs are symbols of children and I interpreted this as meaning that, as God's children, He protects us.

The timing of these religious encounters puzzles me. Why did they occur when they did? Why not years ago, in 1976 or 1980—during one of the many other times I was depressed? Was it because I was so susceptible to suicide during the time they did occur? I have not experienced another religious incident since that year, but I think about them often; and when I was so severely ill in Mississippi in 2000, memories of these religious experiences helped sustain me.

During the years that followed I either witnessed or felt other religious events, but none was of the magnitude of those during 1985-1986. While visiting Our Lady of the Meadows church in Pueblo, Colorado during August of 1987, I watched Jesus on the cross while I prayed. His mouth seemed to speak words I did not hear. The mouth would then be still only to move again after it had stopped. This happened on two other occasions during that same month. I don't know if I imagined these events or if they, in fact, really did happen. What I do know was that each was consoling at a time when I was in despair.

Near the end of that August, a good friend called me one morning to relay a dream she had had the previous night. Lorraine told me that God came to her in the dream and said He had chosen me (Ann) as "a special person" and that I had been given "special graces." He requested of me that I pray the rosary and say novenas...and that I "will be the pillar of strength to my family because of the cross I was bearing." Lorraine added that Jesus wanted me to return to the Catholic Church.

I found this prophetic since I had been visiting nearby Catholic Churches most of that summer and had recently accepted a first grade teaching position at John Neumann Catholic School in Pueblo. Perhaps the message had validity.

In Denver I attend the Church of the Risen Christ on Monaco Street. A beautiful white stone statue of Christ stands high in the courtyard. Around it are several stone benches. There is a familiarity as I look up into the face of the statue. I have seen Christ in the same white robe standing behind me in the small bedroom in State College, Pennsylvania. It is the same figure I saw at the end of a long tunnel when He clearly spoke to me at the chapel on the Penn State campus in 1986 and, again, when He lovingly held out His arms to lambs that were gathered around Him. The church has erected a meditation chapel for parishioners to use for reflection and prayer. I use it from time to time, but the familiarity of the stone benches will not easily be replaced. I am certain that this is where I will continue to sit...under that statue that has provided me so much comfort for so many years.

CHAPTER 17:
Communication

SNAPSHOT
Denver, Colorado Summer 2006

Everyone needs a sounding board and a good communicator when depressed for long time periods. I believe it is imperative to your survival. The distortion of reality is so severe, the world so unbalanced that a rational view of what is happening is necessary.

Communication with others was one of my most important coping strategies. It became the center of my ability to function. It didn't matter that I talked openly with only four people—my two lifelines, Gary and Dr. Sandy Macdonald in State College, Carole Crawford in Pueblo, and Dr. Jon Bell years later in Denver. Each has played a huge role in my ability to survive.

CONSISTENT ENCOURAGEMENT

On days when I awoke depressed, Gary would often spend an hour or so talking with me before leaving for work. He also would call several times throughout the day and spend time with me in the evening. He would reassure me over and over that I needed to believe that I could get through the day and would remind me of all the good things in our lives.

I would respond by telling him how hopeless it all seemed and how I was convinced that the depression would never leave. He would remind me that I had believed this many times before and that, like all those times, I would once again feel good.

Intellectually, I realized he was right. The depression *had* always passed. Previous episodes had faded as fast as they had appeared. Why would this time be any different?

During our conversations, the exasperating part for Gary was that he would have to verbalize the same things over and over. All of this required much patience on his part. He might, for instance, suggest that I write more often in my journal or make an emergency appointment with Sandy.

Gary: "But you have to go to the school program. Susan is counting on you to be there."

Ann: "There is no way...how can I do it? I am so wired. People will talk to me and then I'll not be able to respond intelligently."

Gary: "Arrive close to the time of the program and sit on the end or in the back."

Ann: "What if there are no seats left? Should I go early and try to be obscure? I just know I'll see someone who will want to talk. I just can't."

Gary: "Ann, you can do it. It's something you have to do. Your absence would be obvious and Susan would be upset if you didn't come.

Ann: "I'll try, but do you think I should go early or late? What if someone does want to talk?"

This might go on for five or ten minutes, just this conversation. Hard to believe, isn't it, but these types of conversations were frequent.

When the Old Ann was back, though, I was just the opposite...confident, talkative and laughing, upbeat all the time. And it was hard for this people person to believe all of this. Hard to imagine that I couldn't decide what time to go to a school program, where to sit or how to interact with others. These are things that you automatically "just do." You don't dissect them over and over. Mental illness is so bizarre that it's hard to believe the same person could display such thoughts and actions; or that the same person might be one way in the morning and the other in the afternoon on the very same day. Sadly, this is the case.

I knew my view of the world was skewed. The reality in which I found myself was a far different world than the one in which I am when I am not depressed, and even though I knew that what was outside of me was the world as I had once known it, *my* world was an entirely different one.

* * *

Ironically, *not* sharing my problems with others enabled me to have some semblance of a normal life. I used to believe that if others were to know, I would be less of a person in their eyes and my work would be constantly judged. As a matter of fact, I worked so hard at this deception, I should have gotten a medal.

I had another good reason: back in the seventies, depression was not talked about and was considered more of a mystery than an illness that could be treated. Shame was associated with it. I already believed that I was incompetent and didn't want others to believe the same. I have no doubt that many people not only attached weakness and disgrace to those who were depressed, they were convinced that such people would never be quite the same again.

So, I had good reasons for my reticence.

I had a friend, Joan Fenton, who knew that I was seeing Sandy. I don't remember why I told her, but I remember that she knew. She worked as an admissions counselor at Penn State. I called her one day while I was working at the Foundation. I was very depressed and told her about my mood. I must have sounded pretty bad.

"Call Sandy, Annie," she encouraged. "Call him right now and then let me know what he says."

I hung up, called him and he fit me into his schedule for 3:30 that afternoon. I felt tremendous relief. Making an appointment when I needed one was just another source of hope. Reputable therapists recognize the importance of being available, and are accommodating. They are well aware of the severe depression and feelings of panic and anxiety that are so prevalent during severe episodes.

When I came out of my session, Joan was sitting in the waiting room. I was incredibly touched that she had been concerned about me and had left work to wait for me. I will never forget the kindness that she demonstrated that afternoon. She knew that I was going, but she went one step further, and it was this step that has made my friendship with Joan even more special than it already was. Her presence spoke volumes about her caring and concern for me.

COMMUNICATION UNRAVELS INNER CONFUSION

My therapists provided me with a professional view of this illness and were an important part of my communication. Competent mental health providers understand what I am going through and their suggestions, opinions and assistance have been invaluable. But Sandy was truly a lifeline—a communicator who truly understood me.

SNAPSHOT
State College, Pennsylvania Fall 1976 – summer 1986

Sandy MacDonald is an important person in my life. He knows my thoughts, fears, feelings of inadequacy as well as disappointments, regrets and despair. He knows me, the part of me that is hidden from everyone else.

I knew from the first day that I met Sandy that he was exactly what he presented himself to be. He is a professional who has been there to provide direction, to help me determine where I wanted to take myself. He has given me hope when I had none, order when my life was chaotic.

Sandy has listened to my thoughts and fears. He has helped me make sense of my life when it no longer contained any. He has always been available, making a place for me in his schedule. Most important, he has been my friend.

Sometimes I would be feeling great the day I was to see Sandy and would think about canceling an appointment. I would question the necessity of going, particularly since it was tempting to use that time to do other things. Most often, though, I would resist the temptation and go to my scheduled appointment. I needed that communication.

Sandy would praise all the strides I had made since our previous session, so I would feel very good about myself. Because I knew that I almost always benefited from our talks, and also knew I could never predict whether or not my time would be well spent, I recognized the importance of going even when I felt like canceling.

As years went by I discussed feelings with several close relatives and friends, although not to the extent that I did with my two main confidants. Today, I am very open about my battles. I believe that I can be an inspiration to others and I know that, often, I am.

CHAPTER 18:
Journal Writing

AN EARLY JOURNAL ENTRY...
State College, Pennsylvania November 19, 1974

Have had many urgings to release my thoughts...but no time to do so. It should not be so, but remains a fact. Time seems to dominate. What must life be like for those who allow it to do so completely?

The past few months have left me feeling depressed; dull days filled with rain and clouds seem to adequately reflect all that is in my mind. Life is short, routine if we allow it to be; such routine becomes monotonous and each day becomes much like the previous one.

Change sustains me and makes me feel useful. Underneath all of the uncertainty is the realization that my security is with Gary. I hope he knows how important he is to me, yet, I know that he often doesn't. He experiences feelings of doubt as far as my love for him is concerned. I'm torn between feigning satisfaction for his security and being honest for my own.

As the sky brightens, so do my spirits. Hopefully, this will continue, but I would detest complete acceptance of my life. Frustrations and desire for something different create, I think, a more completeness of me, a realization of the kind of person I am. At least it provides a beginning...

Journal writing has been an excellent tool for me to express myself. The advantage that journaling has over verbal communication is that it requires no appointment and can be accomplished alone and at any time. If I am not at home, but want to write down a particular thought, I have often done this on bank deposit slips, sticky notes or, on numerous occasions, napkins. I would then transfer what was written into my journal once I was home.

None of my journals contain entries written during times when I was not going through a depressive period. The reason for this is that I had no desire to do so, maybe because it was just so joyful to feel good. The journal was a crucial tool I used when depressed...no need to pull it out at any other time. It became a vehicle for relieving stress and provided me a sense of direction, not only for the future, but also often for the day of which an entry was written.

A FAVORITE PLACE FOR WRITING

The bedroom in our State College home was in the basement, a bit below ground level so, other than a picture window facing north, there were no other natural light sources. I loved it down there because the darkness provided a feeling of coziness and security. I usually wrote after Susan and Dave were in bed, and often when Gary was asleep beside me and I would have the light down low. But sometimes I would sit on the end of the bed or propped against two pillows in early afternoon, writing as I heard the Pennsylvania rains hitting my bedroom window.

Sometimes I would look over recent entries, a validation that all that I was experiencing really was happening. But more often than not, I would just begin to write. After entering the date, I would write until I wanted to stop. Some entries were long and some were short. All of it was me "talking to myself." It provided a time to reflect and to organize the thoughts within my mind that had a habit of being extremely disorganized.

An entry from my journal on one long, dreary Pennsylvania day...

JOURNAL ENTRY
State College, Pennsylvania March 11, 1975

This past month has left me feeling empty, dull days filled with rain and clouds. It seems an adequate description of my mind. Each day is the same...my mood corresponding to what I see outside. There is no color, just gray everywhere. My depression favors no season.

MY PEN…AN IMPETUS FOR ENCOURAGEMENT

I used my writing as a mechanism for encouragement, striving for optimism.

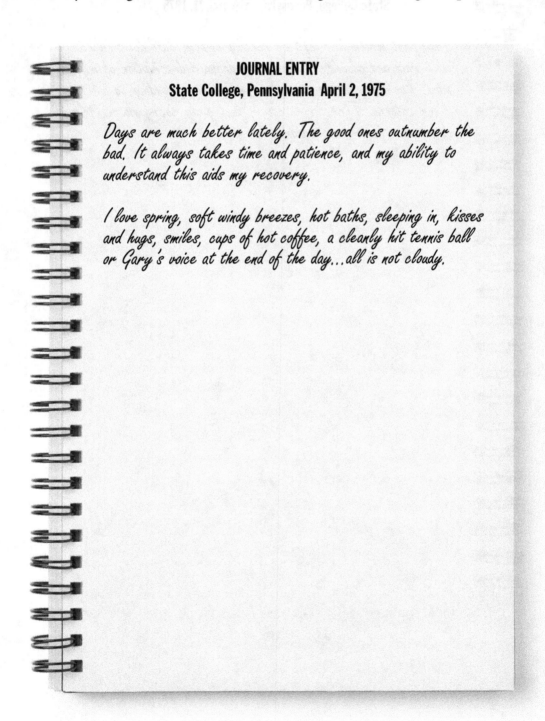

JOURNAL ENTRY
State College, Pennsylvania April 2, 1975

Days are much better lately. The good ones outnumber the bad. It always takes time and patience, and my ability to understand this aids my recovery.

I love spring, soft windy breezes, hot baths, sleeping in, kisses and hugs, smiles, cups of hot coffee, a cleanly hit tennis ball or Gary's voice at the end of the day…all is not cloudy.

Writing enables me to look at my life objectively. It serves as an incentive to have a better day tomorrow and is a reminder of the progress I have made, be it ever so insignificant.

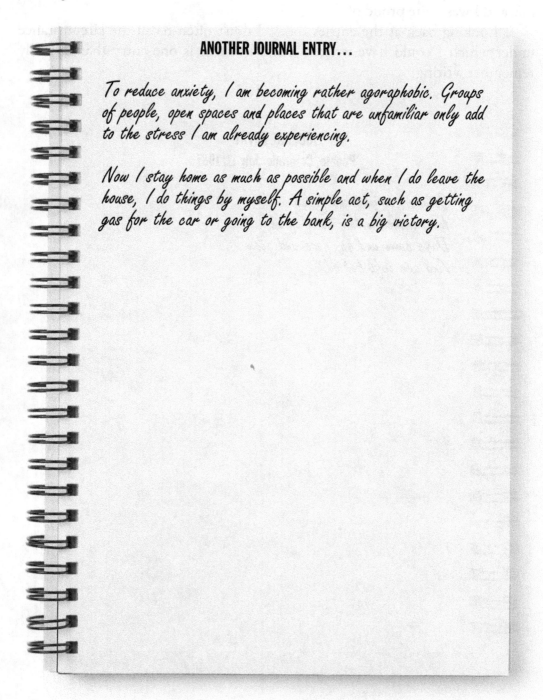

ANOTHER JOURNAL ENTRY...

To reduce anxiety, I am becoming rather agoraphobic. Groups of people, open spaces and places that are unfamiliar only add to the stress I am already experiencing.

Now I stay home as much as possible and when I do leave the house, I do things by myself. A simple act, such as getting gas for the car or going to the bank, is a big victory.

I would record such events in my journal at the end of the day and that in itself was motivation for me to complete such activities. I never felt that accomplishing small things was insignificant because I knew that they were major events for me, and I was quite proud of them.

Looking back at the entries today, I don't often recall the circumstance under which I could have written them. But this is one entry that I vividly remember writing:

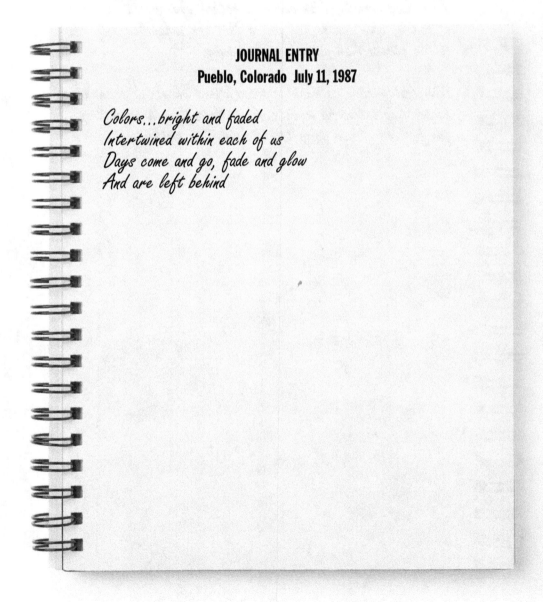

JOURNAL ENTRY
Pueblo, Colorado July 11, 1987

Colors...bright and faded
Intertwined within each of us
Days come and go, fade and glow
And are left behind

I felt extremely sad that day. I viewed life as futile, and saw the colors that inter-twine themselves in our world as being representative of elation and despair, both of which were very much a part of me. Just as days endlessly come and go, so do our emotions, only to be left behind...no longer a part of us. Depression does this; it makes me feel as if my life is futile; and, if my life is pointless, so am I.

The depressive bouts I have suffered can be tracked as I read through my journals. The entries help me remember how far down I was at that particular time. Even though I had experienced depression off and on since 1974, I had never had a depressive "breakdown" until 1984. But I already had a long history with my journal.

A GOOD RATING SYSTEM

Dr. Alan Feiger, my Denver psychiatrist during the academic year of 1984-85, suggested that, on a scale of minus five to plus five, I write down the appropri-ate number as an indicator of what kind of day I'd had. I found this suggestion to be quite helpful. It allowed me to see progress made or lost when I went back over the journal entries. Days with depression go much more slowly than those without. At the end of a bad day I would feel as if the darkness had encased me for a much longer time than it actually had. I might give such a day a −4 and feel as if I will never move toward recovery. But looking back at previous days might indicate that this was just the first bad day in the past week. This rating system provided an accurate assessment of just how far I had slipped back or how much I had improved.

I sometimes used other journaling strategies as well. I would write pep talks to inspire and motivate myself. I would use repetition to reinforce a point:

I can do this. I can do this. I can do this.

Just writing it provided determination. Sometimes I would break the pencil point because I would be pressing so hard on the page. Each episode, as well as each day with this illness, differs from all the others. That's the way this depression is...so completely unpredictable. My journal writing has been used for reflecting, for analyzing myself, for rating my days as well as for encourage-ment. It has been an integral part of my return to sanity each time.

* * *

One day Gary and I were cleaning out the storage area in our basement here in Denver when he came across the box that contained books about depression and all the journals I had kept until that time. I was still teaching and was tossing out many professional materials that were out of date.

"What's in that box?" I inquired.

"Just some books about depression and your old journals," Gary responded. "You aren't writing in them any more. They're some of your first ones. Why don't you just throw them away?"

I remember the sinking feeling I had in my stomach as if it was just yesterday.

Throw them away? Throw them away? Why, I could never throw them away because those words on those pages chronicle the despair, the physical and mental pain felt so deeply and also the many words of encouragement I provided at times I so desperately needed it. Those words are *me*, telling myself that all of the pain is worth it...just hang on, hang in there...telling myself that my world will once again right itself, and I will once again be happy.

The journals remain.

CHAPTER 18:
Educating Yourself

SNAPSHOT
State College, Pennsylvania Fall of 1976

I don't know how many times I have listened to the tel-med tapes. I'm glad that Centre Community Hospital provides the service. I think that I have those tapes memorized. I listen to them again and again. Each time I hear them, though, I am again reminded that what I am experiencing is common enough that they have a tape about it. I guess that misery does love company.

Ever since the day I was diagnosed as having depression, I have immersed myself in everything I could find to read on the subject. Each time a book comes out that has received a good review I would either purchase it or check it out of the library. This is not to say that I read everything on the subject because I don't.

Some of the books out there are not informative while others are way too simplistic. Writers in the medical profession write many, and, while they are certainly educational, many of these authors are writing from a professional rather than a personal position. I use such books to gain information about medication even though I would never make a decision based solely on the information provided in a book.

Most books written by those in the profession are written for the general public rather than for colleagues, so the content is easily grasped. Many are focused on the use of antidepressants or how to cope with the illness without medication. But, while these books are informative, you often come away convinced that the authors have never experienced depression's pain. It is important that you have some idea of a book's worth before you decide to read it. You certainly want to trust the author's knowledge and experience.

I recommend *Feeling Good* by Dr. David Burns. (David D. Burns, MD. *Feeling Good: The New Mood Therapy*. New York: Avon Books, 1980) The pages of his book contain eye-opening information. Gary and I knew nothing about the specifics of depression, and this was our first step to educating ourselves. I honestly believe that self-education is one of the best things you can do to help yourself get through the dread. I am also convinced that you need to be very analytical about all of the reading that you do. It's not enough just to read the words. You need to apply them to your particular situation and any questions that might arise must be further investigated...

What are the statistics of certain symptoms? How many people are able to recover without taking medication? Are there therapies or strategies the author suggests that might be helpful amidst those that might not? These are some of the questions you need to ask yourself if you are to get the maximum benefits. It's hard work (it got easier when the Internet became available), but, for me, it was therapeutic in itself. And for someone who loves learning, it's also very satisfying.

The books I find most interesting are those written by people who have personally experienced this illness. It is these authors with whom I can most closely identify. I have felt the horrific symptoms they describe and I, like they, have struggled to cope. Much of what they convey is verification of how I have suffered; and just knowing that others feel out of control, are unable to put words into sentences or wonder if all of the pain is worth the struggle confirms many of the fears I have experienced. It is also good to know that other people have questioned their capabilities just as I have often questioned mine.

I read books that spoke to life and life's struggles, finding them inspirational and understanding that down times often result in making us better people. I have found this to be true. The Bible has passages that seem to "speak" to us, providing hope.

The Road Less Traveled first appeared on the market in 1978 and I read it soon after. (M. Scott Peck. *The Road Less Traveled: A New Psychology of Love, Traditional Values and Spiritual Growth*. New York: Simon & Schuster, Inc., 1978.) It is an amazing book and continues to be my favorite. I've read it innumerable times; I have given many copies to others as gifts and have two copies myself. Authored by M. Scott Peck, a psychiatrist educated at Harvard (BA) and Case Western Reserve (MD), it challenges the reader to give much thought to not only her/his life, but to life in general.

"Life is difficult" is the first sentence of the book, and these three words hit me hard upon seeing them for the first time.

"My life certainly is", I thought as I absorbed the words.

And then I delved into the rest of Peck's content in which he goes on to explain that it is the difficulties we face that makes us strong and provides determination. It made no sense to me back in 1978.

"Who wants to go through all of this, and just how strong will it make me"? I remember thinking rather sarcastically.

The author also discusses the importance of delaying gratification, accomplishing the unpleasant tasks before we experience the pleasure. "It is," says Peck, "the only way to live". We have all done some of this...homework before play when we were growing up; working hard at our jobs makes the weekend that much sweeter, etc.

I viewed the ups and downs of my life in much the same way. Feeling good was *far* better when feeling badly preceded it. In my case, I often delayed gratification for an extremely long time, but I would then exhilarate in those good times. And during the years of short episodes of severe depression followed by parts of days or weeks at a time of returning to my old self, the good days were simply wonderful.

I have personally experienced much of what Peck espouses. Each time I recovered...which often took months and, one time, close to eighteen months... I was stronger and much more determined; and the delaying of gratification, though mine was an involuntary delay, resulted in glorious times.

Reading ideas and suggestions from others often provides more tools that I can implement. Depression is, quite frankly, a constant battle that continually changes.

Over the years, Gary and I would usually buy two copies of recommended books, read them together and then discuss them. We found that this was the most effective way to help us both understand. If only one spouse is involved in learning all the details of the illness and therapies, it becomes difficult if not impossible to make joint decisions and share feelings.

As an example, a good friend of mine was having marital problems and she and her husband also went to see Sandy for help. After several sessions she told me that they had hoped to get more out of the sessions. They were discouraged because they had expected Sandy to provide specific answers for them. Their idea of therapy was to explain what was wrong in the marriage and to have Sandy provide immediate feedback that would tell them how they could solve the problems they were having. In addition, while my friend was doing all the recommended reading, her husband was not.

Predictably, the counseling was not as effective as it would have been had the three of them been able to discuss the assigned readings. It was essential that they both were committed to doing all that they could to achieve optimal benefit. Since this was not happening, they decided not to continue in therapy.

* * *

Being a consummate reader, I like to browse the depression/medication sections of libraries, Borders, Barnes & Noble and Denver's Tattered Cover Book Store. There I will pull books off the shelves, find a good easy chair and perhaps spend hours, just sitting and reading or taking notes. The availability of the Internet provides even more opportunity. You are able to search for books on specific subjects and can often look at the table of contents, back page and excerpts from chapters should you so choose.

Each time major depression would return, I'd find I was drawn to *Darkness Visible*. Written by the famous author, William Styron, this small book delivers a huge message (William Styron. *Darkness Visible: A Memoir of Madness*. New York: Vintage Books, 1990). Subtitled *A Memoir of Madness*, it is, indeed, just that. Like so many, Styron grappled with the overpowering urge to commit suicide. Beautifully written, his words go directly to the core.

"Oh, my God. That's it exactly!" I found myself gasping. I was astounded that his words were mine, his feelings and emotions the same.

Familiarizing myself with every aspect of this disease validated my symptoms. It made me feel "normal" even though I knew I wasn't. I guess it made me feel like I was "normally depressed." I made certain that I was up on what was "in" and why it was a better medication choice than what was "out." Articles espousing the benefits of exercise were scrutinized, television programs or movies about mental illness were viewed and all of what I learned was discussed not only with Gary but also with Sandy Macdonald and, later, my other therapists.

TAKING A LOOK AT ALTERNATIVE THERAPIES

I often outright rejected or only partially accepted many of the medical conjectures concerning recovery. One of them was a theory developed in the sixties by Dr. Aaron Beck, a doctor at the University of Pennsylvania School of Medicine. He called his ideas and treatment techniques "thinking therapy," better known as "cognitive therapy." (David D. Burns, MD. *Feeling Good: The New Mood Therapy*. New York: Avon Books, 1980)

Cognitive therapy espouses that those who are depressed are in that state because of negative thinking. It is this negative thinking that needs to be addressed before the mood of the patient can begin to improve. But who can say what came first? Was it the negative thinking or the depression? One thing is certain...where you find depression, you will also find negative thinking.

In *Feeling Good*, Dr. Burns explains this "new mood therapy." (Burns 1980) It is his belief that many people who take antidepressants do not need them; they can significantly improve their mood by implementing cognitive thinking techniques. Dr. Burns *does* feel that there are those for whom medication is necessary, but, in the case of many, he believes this is not true.

Many people do not want to take medication for religious or a variety of other valid reasons. They would be candidates for theories or ideas on how to improve mood sans antidepressants.

I do believe that there is truth to "mind over matter," i.e., those who tend to be morose tend to also experience low moods, but negative thinking is not necessarily depression. I am certain that some who *are* depressed can work through it by applying Dr. Beck's exercises, but I staunchly believe that, while I incorporate cognitive therapy techniques on a daily basis, it is not the entire answer for me. In working with five therapists and three family physicians over the past thirty years, the conclusion has always been that my depression is due to chemical imbalance within my brain. Regardless of depression's cause, however, cognitive therapy techniques can be extremely beneficial, something I often discovered during times when my illness was not severe.

While I am no expert in this field (although I feel as if I am!), I would think that the fact that I can be severely depressed in the morning only to have it dissipate by afternoon would indicate that it is chemical rather than situational. I can move from suicidal into loving life and back again within short time periods.

THINKING POSITIVELY

I have used many of the exercises of cognitive therapy and found them most helpful. I have always made positive suggestions to myself, counted my blessings and given myself credit for having a good day or accomplishing things. These are considered cognitive therapy. Giving pep talks to yourself and silently rationalizing when things have not turned out as you had hoped are other helpful techniques.

I also would talk myself through self-criticism. An example would be the following:

Negative thinking: We made this move because of me. It is I who has let everyone down. I am solely to blame.

Cognitive Thinking: I was severely depressed when we made the decision. All I wanted was to get well. How helpful is it to everyone for me to be that way? We made what we thought was the right decision at that time.

Although the cognitive therapy theory does not fully apply to my case, I found it of interest and helpful. There is certainly some validity in it, and I know that its application has helped millions. By changing your thinking, you can often improve your mood. Many who find cognitive therapy to be successful are not severely depressed, while others who are may experience a degree of mood improvement. If my depression was mild, I was able to feel better by incorporating cognitive therapy techniques. But, if the depression was too severe, it did absolutely nothing to improve my mind. I had to have medication.

THE LATE THIRTIES GROUP

In the seventies, during the time of my on again-off again depressive bouts, I was struggling with issues that centered around my purpose in life. Perhaps it was due to thinking about mortality since all of my peers knew that death was right around the corner from age forty! I was in a support group comprised of women in their late thirties. Support groups were "the thing" at that time. I was thirty-seven years old.

Many women were questioning their contentment, or lack of. The time period was one during which women were just beginning to emerge from the shadows of their husbands. They were being noticed as separate entities. Party conversations began to center around our goals or aspirations rather than our parenting or to whom we were married. It was a welcome change, but one that caused us to ask ourselves and one another, "OK, now what?"

We called ourselves The Late Thirties Group...all of us struggling with what direction we wanted to take our lives. We wanted a purpose, something that was "ours" rather than a spin off of what came from something or someone else.

I loved the group. Each of us had her own issues. Some of the women were unhappy in their marriages while others were considering career changes. I fell into the latter group, feeling restless and discontent.

We met for a ten-week period and continued meeting informally after that time. I became friends with a couple of the women, but each of us was a crucial part of the group. The support we gave one another was helpful. We exchanged books and information, we were empathetic and made sure to give equal time to each group member. We all felt that the experience was definitely a positive one.

LIKE THE STAGES OF GRIEF

Educating myself on this illness has made me aware of the similarities between the stages that individuals go through when they are grieving and what I have experienced when I am depressed. Looking at the big picture of the past thirty-some years, I am able to identify specific "stages" as it became apparent that I was in the midst of deep depression. When people experience grief, it is because of a loss, such as death of a loved one, empty-nest syndrome or loss of a job. I was grieving the loss of my mental health.

THE STAGES OF MY DEPRESSION

- **Denial** is the first stage of depression. I spent the first two years of my experience with this illness in this stage. Given that denial may or may not be recognized for what it is, I spent all this time convinced that I was merely experiencing discontentment. As time went by and I was further away from the life I had once known, my denial was recognized and the second stage of my fight for sanity emerged.

- **Acknowledgment** began the day I sat in my den and was stunned with the realization that it was depression from which I was suffering and that I desperately needed help.

- The second stage quickly moves into the third, that of **acceptance**. Once I admitted that I was mentally ill, it was not difficult for me to accept the diagnosis. This stage appears every time depression reappears and, during this time, I once again do all that I have to do to work through each bout.

> - I see the fourth stage as one of **maintenance**, knowing that I have to always work to maintain my sanity. Maintenance is ongoing and consists of implementing the numerous coping strategies and techniques that have been of help to me as I have recovered each time. I will *never* leave this stage because what I am maintaining is my life, with or without depression. Continuing to take antidepressants and see my therapists on a regular schedule are two of the things that I do to maintain my mental health. In a sense, they are preventative.

I left anger off the list, one of the typical stages of grief, because I cannot say that I have ever been angry about the fact that I have suffered from this affliction. I have been crestfallen, frustrated and distraught, but I have never been angry. You or someone you know with depression might experience anger though, and it is good to admit this. It is my opinion that each of us reacts in different ways and goes through somewhat different stages before recovery is reached. These are the stages that I have experienced.

SHARING MY DOUBTS, FEARS AND TRIUMPHS

I think that probably the first time I was able to openly discuss my depression was in the late eighties when we moved to Pueblo. Even then I only discussed it with family, though not in great detail.

The main reason for this delay (twenty years certainly is a long delay) was public acceptance of mental illness in general. Until I was "stricken" (what a word), I thought that there was no hope for those who were "mentally ill." Politicians and other people in the public eye who suffered from depression were ostracized, often to the point of professional ruin. Sounds hard to believe, but this was the way it was. Even later, when facts about depression started surfacing, you were horrified if you heard that someone you actually knew was under the care of a psychiatrist, taking medication or both. You felt sorry for them, shame for their family and you steered clear when you saw them at your children's school or elsewhere in the community.

With time, the public stigma slowly began to lessen. For many, however, personal embarrassment for yourself or others remains. If someone feels embarrassed about his or her depression, blame it on lack of education and/or unwillingness to have an open mind about mental illness.

Recently, when situations have presented themselves, I have openly discussed my struggles with others who have either personally experienced the illness or have someone close to them who has. Believe me, it is comforting to know that someone you know can tell you firsthand what they have gone through. I try to do this when it seems pertinent because I think it gives much hope to others.

Sharing techniques that have helped me, suggesting books that I have found useful and just letting someone else know that I understand what they are experiencing makes me feel that I can be of great help to others. It always astounds others when they discover my mental health history because I am now such a together person. I know that they gain a lot of hope just knowing that if I could get through all of it and function as well as I do today, they might well be able to do the same. In fact, that is why I wrote this book.

EDUCATION IS CONTINUOUS

These days I am able to continue to educate myself in the field of depression through a variety of media. I saw the movie, *A Beautiful Mind*, the life story of John Nash, the brilliant mathematician who was awarded the Nobel Prize in Economics in 1994 for his work on game theory. (Sylvia Nasar. *A Beautiful Mind: A Biography of John Forbes Nash. Jr.* New York: Simon and Schuster, 1998) Nash began his descent into madness at age thirty as he began to hallucinate. He maintained that aliens were communicating with him, he imagined people who did not exist and he became so delusional that he spent three decades in and out of mental hospitals.

Diagnosed with paranoid schizophrenia, Nash was awarded the Nobel Prize soon after he began to emerge from his delusional existence. The movie is about the story of his life, a brilliant man whose mind severely cracked and remained that way for many of his adult years.

Director Ron Howard did a brilliant job illustrating this when it was revealed that Nash's roommate never existed, nor did the child who appeared at various times. I was astonished when I realized this. It seemed so real, and this is exactly the way those who have this mental illness see their world. To them, these imaginary people are real. In much the same way, my distortions of reality *are* real.

When I saw the movie and when I read books about others who have mental illnesses that involve hearing voices or seeing people that are not there, I am always thankful. I breathe a sigh of relief, reminding myself that things could have been far worse for me. We all do this—rationalizing when things are not good that they could be much worse.

I continue to talk with others who have been afflicted. Since I am much more open about what I have endured, I know that I have been helpful. I am particularly interested in the subject of suicide. It is prevalent among the young and the elderly and has almost been "romanticized" by the recent school shootings.

While I know that those who manage to complete their death wish no longer suffer, I am cognizant of the fact that those left behind inherit that suffering. These are the people who beat themselves up over the fact that they might have been able to prevent it from happening, but I know differently. Did I mention this before? **No one** can prevent a loved one from committing suicide.

I can't remember specific television programs I have watched, but if anything about depression or antidepressant medication appears on 20/20 or similar programs, I put it on my calendar. I love to watch interviews of those who had conquered this illness. I remember one in particular long ago when Dick Cavett was interviewed. He was one of the early ones to bring his personal story to the public. Oprah often has programs focused on the illness, as do Larry King and Dr. Phil. Recently, 60 Minutes profiled a new surgery that may help people with severe depression not helped with medication.

It is my belief that the more you absorb, the better off you are. If I gain nothing from the program in the way of information, I have always gained validity of my journey. Sometimes I can identify with what is being discussed, other times I think the information is out in left field, but I work at keeping well informed.

Somewhere in between the time that depression was not at all accepted and years later when it was finally considered an ailment from which one could recover, I started to open up to others about my struggle. I had a passion to help others cope with the horror of this illness. That passion remains. The reaction often is amazement because these people have a difficult time believing that they can be "their old selves" once again. Those who are familiar with what all of it is about, though, realize that once your life is righted, the person you once were returns in time. You never *truly* return as the person you once were, however, because that is an impossibility. If it were possible to see deep inside those of us who have recovered, our differences would be apparent. And I would add that the differences are to the good: we have more depth, more caring and inspiration, and our priorities have changed completely.

CHAPTER 20:
Exercise and Healthy Choices

Running, running, running...from reality and responsibiity, catching a few moments of clean pleasure and freedom. Hidden and surface thoughts are clarified, bringing me face to face with myself.

It gives me personal space, time to question and reflect. With each mile, my mind is clearer, and I am a more complete person.

Exercise, one of the least expensive of my therapies, has been an imperative component of my recovery. Throughout the years, running, tennis and weightlifting have been at the top of my list. When I was first experiencing depression, I started running. My routine was much the same each day, and by the end of my run, my mood would be stable. The heavy sinking feeling with which I awoke would usually be gone, and I would shower and dress. I would feel much better the remainder of the day.

I remember when I'd completed a mile for the first time. It was winter, and ice covered the roads, so I went to Recreation Hall on the Penn State campus to use its running track. The rest of the family went to the Unitarian Fellowship that morning. When I was finished running, back at the Unitarian Fellowship with flushed face, I was heartily congratulated by Gary and other fellow runners. It wasn't long before I was running two, three, then four miles each time I went out so I quickly realized how insignificant a mile is to one who routinely runs, but I knew that it was anything but insignificant to me.

During dark days I would make myself begin to walk first, then jog, and quite often I picked up speed before I returned home. Once you get past the stiffness and into the rhythm of a run, it becomes easy. Sometimes you feel as if you could go forever. There is truth to the term endorphin high, commonly known as "runners' high."

Knowing that I *should* run and actually *doing* it were two different things. It is not easy to move, let alone run around blocks for an extended period of time when this illness takes over. So I would *make* myself do whatever it took to get going...put on running shorts, put on socks, put on tennis shoes, get out the door, begin walking to the corner, slowly quickening my pace until I would realize that the darkness was beginning to lift a bit.

Sometimes it was very, very hard, but I was usually able to convince myself that I would be glad once I got going. But, with the same sinking feeling each morning, faced with the same hesitancies each and every day, it took energy and will power of which I had very little.

Tennis was another type of exercise for me and it helped my depression too. After a set or two I would feel like the old Ann and I would be ready to take on the remainder of the day knowing that I had to take full advantage of these times when I could function. Anything that needed to be done, as well as things that didn't but I nevertheless wanted to do, could be accomplished in record time. When one experiences the terrible feeling that depression creates, feeling great is pure luxury, and I would bask in that feeling. I dreaded going to bed those nights, however, because I knew I might be in for another battle when I awoke the next morning and I would have to gain the strength necessary to go through my exercise routine all over again.

Tennis is also a wonderful way to work off stress, and I played several times a week. The humidity of Pennsylvania made it uncomfortable, but I loved the sweaty feeling while running after balls. I had only one partner who, like me, loved to play in the middle of the day. Betz Hanley was a professor in the College of Physical Education and a wonderful tennis player. We jumped at the chance to play in the heat of the day, and in Pennsylvania heat and humidity go together. We'd come off the court wringing wet, happy as clams, and drink cold cans of grape soda as we lazed around in the lounge chairs. Those were the days.

JOURNAL ENTRY
State College, Pennsylvania Race Day
July 9, 1978

Arts' Festival ten miles run – big goal for the year accomplished. A mixture of emotions...relief being the main one, but also elation.

Physically I felt well—miles two through seven were super—shoulders and neck ached. Last mile was the most difficult. It seemed endless, but it was bearable; much more comfortable than I had anticipated.

Next year I'll work on my time! (I was racer number 500. I placed 414th with a time of 103 minutes).

My 1978 New Year's Resolutions were to run the ten-mile Arts Festival Race as well as to run a total of one thousand miles. I trained for the race until mid-July, when I accomplished my first goal, hitting the street six or seven days a week and recording the number of miles run on back pages of my journal. These two goals provided incentives, a definite purpose each day and, when I recorded the number of miles I had run, it gave me an exhilarating feeling. Such a little thing...a number...but it was a huge thing to me as, I am certain, it would be to others who are aware of how this illness is so capable of sapping energy.

The completion of this race was a huge goal. Gary realized this more than anyone else because he knew what I faced on a daily basis. I was confident that I could complete the ten miles because I had trained so consistently. I had heard that if I completed five to six miles every now and then, I would be able to run the entire ten. I am not aware of whose theory this is, or whether there is any truth to it, but believing it worked for me.

SNAPSHOT
Race Day

The siren sounds and we are off. The first three miles are flat and there is no shade, but I am not yet tired and am caught up in the excitement.

The gravel makes a crunching sound underneath my running shoes.

I begin to heat up, and enjoy talking with a fellow runner before she speeds ahead of me.

We begin winding through immense shade trees, and the coolness is a welcome relief. Race assistants along the course hand small paper cups filled with water to extended hands. I feel good as I psych myself up for the last three miles.

Taking a sharp right turn, I am on Route 45, the highway coming into town.

Intense heat beats down on me…I am drenched in a mixture of spilled water and summer sweat.

It becomes apparent that what appears to be level ground has a slight upgrade. The uphill finish is difficult and I think that reversing the course might be a very good idea for next year's race.

It seems as if I will never reach the edge of campus, each step more of an effort than the previous one. As Route 45 becomes College Avenue, I breathe a sigh of relief, aware that I have only a half-mile to cover before I reach the finish.

The uphill grade does not lessen, but cool air refreshes as I run past massive trees that line the street.

The final turn veers right, up the sidewalk where family and friends cheer on the runners. I spot Gary, Susan and Dave standing under a shade tree. They are smiling, and so am I.

I will always remember the three of them standing there as I walked toward them. It was obvious that they were proud of me and, before I could say a word, Dave handed me a small paper bag.

"This is for you, Mom."

I knelt down beside my eight-year-old smiling, freckled-face son. Inside the bag was a tan plastic bear and written across a sign that was being held by the bear were the words: World's Greatest Mom.

"I love it, Dave," I said as I hugged him close.

Later that night Gary told me the story of this gift. It seems that he, Susan and Dave were walking very quickly down Allen Street to get to the finish line of the race. He suddenly realized that Dave was no longer with them. This was not unusual, because Dave had a way of disappearing, always running ahead of the rest of us.

Exasperated, he began calling for him when Dave, carrying a small paper bag, suddenly appeared.

"What are you doing? We're late. Hurry!"

It was only when Dave handed his purchase to me that Gary knew the reason for his hasty departure.

On November 29—four months later—I ran my one-thousandth mile for that year. This was a time for celebration of my major goals completed. I was euphoric. The training and the persistence that resulted in reaching those two goals had come in the midst of severe adversity. Only Gary and I knew what amazing accomplishments these were.

My running became so habitual that I felt incomplete when I did not run. I ran in the heat and humidity of the Pennsylvania summer as well as in the bone-chilling cold of winter— sometimes in sub-zero weather. As time-consuming as all of this was, the rewards were worth the effort. It was therapeutic so I kept running.

For several years I was truly addicted to running, as were many others in town. Most everyone was into fitness, with running being a favorite choice for many. Runners could be seen throughout the town, and many people ran every day. You got to know them, despite the fact that you had no idea who they were... just friendly waves as you passed one another. Frank Shorter, the well-known runner, was making headlines and Dr. Kenneth Cooper, also an avid runner, was espousing the benefits. It was not only a healthy activity...it was *the* thing to do, a status thing of sorts.

"Yes, I'm a runner," people would remark to one another at social events, having recognized someone they had seen running around the Penn State golf course. That was where many who worked on campus ran during their lunch hour. You would hurry to change at the Rec Hall locker room, hit the trails, shower and catch a quick lunch at Kern, a nearby campus building. You'd pass friends and acquaintances, exchange "the runner's quick wave" before they passed. "On your left," people would say...the expression to let runners know that they needed to pass you. Yes, those were the days...being one of the elite group was quite satisfying. Aside from the fact that it lifted my mood, the miles I put in were the reason I was so fit.

When I was in the middle of a run one day I remember wondering if I would be exercising all my life. Almost before the question had left my mind, the answer came to me. I knew for certain that exercise would always be a part of my life, particularly if I wanted to remain in good health. This is not to say that I haven't slipped now and then, but slipping is an excellent reminder of how good I do feel when I routinely work out.

When I was stabilized on medication and feeling well, I put in a lot of energy selecting and preparing special meals for the family. I was into the vegetarian phase for about seven years. I made my own peanut butter and yogurt, read Molly Katzen's *Moosewood Cookbook* as if it was the Bible. First published in 1977, the book sells like hot cakes (yes, they do have recipes for hot cakes, four different varieties). I honestly loved the recipes and had great success with them...well, most of them...we still tell the lentil-walnut burger story...

SNAPSHOT
State College, Pennsylvania Winter 1978

Gary, Susan and Dave were pretty much tolerating this vegetarian kick I was on. Now and then they loved what I prepared. Most of the time they thought it was "pretty good."

I know that the dishes weren't their favorites because my daughter apparently mentioned her frustration to my mother when we were in Colorado one August.

"It's just a phase your mother is going through, honey," my mother assured.

Since everyone missed having a hamburger, I was delighted to discover a recipe for lentil-walnut burgers that sounded great.

"What are these?" was the first question I got that evening.

Everyone reluctantly took a bite. I did the same, only to discover that something had gone wrong. These weren't the nutty, firm burgers I thought I had made...they were mushy and rather tasteless. I was to later discover that I had not followed the recipe correctly because they really were nutty and firm when I tried again.

> No one said a word for a minute or two. "Let's all go to Burger King!" I announced. Smiles broke out all around as everyone ran with relief to grab a coat.

Both Gary and I got into reading about and taking vitamin supplements. Seeking advice from experts in that field, we have kept a regimen of eating organic foods that includes grains and seeds on a regular basis. Well, we have taken detours now and then. Lack of energy and just looking in a mirror are reasons enough to know that we need to get back on course. As we have aged, we continue to make appointments with those who are knowledgeable in this field to assure ourselves that we are consuming the right amount of everything. Because theories change, it's important to keep current on all of this.

I loved going to the Dandelion Market, a health food store in State College. You might find it hard to believe, but all this was something that we pretty much kept to ourselves back then, discussing such things only with those people who were on the same wavelength. It was the mid-seventies, and people who ate health foods were "weird"—it was certainly not mainstream, so we kept this, along with the fact that I was not feeling at my best mentally, well under wraps. If people discovered I was "nuts," they would most likely make the leap that it was no wonder that I was into the health kick...I must not be playing with a full deck.

Nautilus gyms became popular in the late seventies so I would lift weights as well. The first time I was introduced to the equipment, the young instructor must have thought I was training for the Olympics because I could hardly move the next morning, and the next and the next.

Along with all of this exercise and vitamin taking came Transcendental Meditation. I think Susan and Dave were ten and six when we decided that TM was for us. It was quite popular at the time but, once again, not with the conventional group. The cost was $100 for TM training and that was a lot of money back then. You really had to believe in its benefits. It was yet another secret of ours. We knew some of those who partook; many fellow Unitarians were into out-of-the-ordinary life-style choices.

So each morning and each night we sat upright in bed leaning against the headboard or on the floor against a wall, silently repeating our mantras to ourselves. You are instructed to never reveal your mantra to anyone and I never have, despite repeated requests from my daughter. Who knows what the repercussions might be?

Our instructor was a young man named Smith. He was meek and rather pasty looking, soft-spoken and "into the TM lingo." Smith showed us how to meditate and, when the time allotted was over, he would always ask all of us, "Did you feel some peace, some calm?" We all remarked that yes, we did.

To the chagrin of each, we enrolled Susan and Dave in TM. Far from being enthusiastic, they, like us, were each given a mantra and were told by Smith, "never reveal it." I remember that the cost for their training was $50 each, still expensive but half the price of ours. I also remember the one day that Dave was arguing with me about something or other and, in anger, threatened to reveal his mantra.... gasp!

On a serious note, though, I think that TM has definite benefits. Using it causes us to slow down, to reflect on nothing but our breathing...it takes us away from all with which we contend on a daily basis. It is, I believe, good for people and I know that it gave me brief time periods away from all that was going on inside my head.

For those who don't exercise routinely, just walking around the block or working in the garden can make a difference in mood. That was my routine when I had my worst depressive episode in Mississippi. I was incredibly weak and could hardly walk across the room, but I managed to pull myself around the neighborhood.

Two years before we moved to Mississippi, we decided to get a dog. With a beautiful park only a block a way, it would be convenient to take it for daily walks. I went to the shelter several times looking for a puppy. Dave called one morning announcing that he had just seen two together in a cage that were border collie mixes. He had chosen the tri-color puppy and suggested I might want to look at the black and white one.

It's not easy to look at a puppy and decide to walk away...she came home with us the following morning. We named her Poco, which means "little one" in Spanish. She was wonderful company and, since we were committed to walking her, we got exercise right along with her.

Sadly, we had to put Poco down due to extreme fear aggression. After months of denial and six slight attacks on petrified people, along with a detailed recommendation from a dog behaviorist in Texas, we knew that we had to do the responsible thing. While we were convinced that there was no choice, it was an incredibly hard decision. Poco had bonded more with me. I was the person she most trusted; yet I was the one responsible for her leaving us forever.

As expected, once I was past the denial period, extreme sadness set in and I deeply felt the emotions that come with missing a dog. I tried to rationalize...

I had tried every angle like keeping her muzzled on walks and locking her in the back rooms when we had company (this failed once when someone left a door open and she angrily, teeth bared, sprang at two children who were visiting). Realizing that nothing is fool proof, this was the incident that caused us to make our decision.

But knowing that you did the right thing is quite separate from missing what is no longer there. I grieved for close to two years, probably because of my susceptibility to depression. And when I hit the bottom five months later, I know that this was one of the things that contributed.

I have always believed that the pain of grief is proportional to what we have lost. The joy of having Poco was well worth the pain of letting her go. I knew that we would eventually get another dog.

Three years later, I brought home the first dog I asked to see at the shelter. Unlike Poco, Chloe was a year and a half (no breaking in another puppy at our age) and her temperament is submissive and low key. We walk her at the park as we exercise right along with her and she is great company.

This is still another form of exercising that is good for not only your physical health, but your mental health as well. People who live alone would benefit from having a pet, and research shows that those who do are happier and live longer.

I cannot overemphasize the benefits of exercise of any kind for everyone. When you work hard at something physical, the benefits cause you to take a close look at other parts of your lifestyle...stress, eating, weight gain, etc. Exercise continues to be an integral part of my life.

CHAPTER 21:
Therapy

SNAPSHOT
State College, Pennsylvania
September 1976

...I continue to sit there, thinking through all that has just become so apparent. I slowly begin to understand my failure to recognize the obvious. I had assumed that a person who suffered a nervous breakdown was insane and would be out of control.

I am not irrational, nor insane or out of control; but I know that I am not normal. I also know that I need help...

In looking back on that day when I sat in my den on Ellen Avenue in State College and finally admitted that I was ill, I can now understand why I failed to get help sooner than I did. I was astonished when I realized that I was in the midst of mental illness.

Mental illness...mental illness...until that moment the words had sounded as if they belonged to someone other than myself. How could I be mentally ill when I was able to function? I got up each day. I got Susan and Dave off to school. I could carry on a conversation (most of the time).

Until that morning I thought I would be able to recognize someone who was mentally ill. He or she would be wacky, bizarre or out of control.

But that day I knew that I had been wrong. I knew that I was mentally ill.

WHY THERAPY IS SO ESSENTIAL

Even though I am convinced that the road to recovery is much quicker when therapy and medication are employed simultaneously, the relief of therapy is much more immediate than that of medication. There are several reasons that this is true. First of all, verbalizing what is happening to you makes you feel better right away. Also, even though it was difficult to put my feelings and fears into words, I knew that I was talking to someone who had counseled many people before me. This is a comforting feeling. My reluctance to verbalize my innermost emotions back then was not only due to embarrassment. It was also due to my inability to adequately describe what depression *feels* like. It is *very* difficult, but I knew that a therapist, more than anyone else, would know this. This provided additional comfort.

Another immediate relief for me was that Sandy was able to suggest ways I might help myself. We discussed the fact that I was keeping a journal and he validated my intentions. He said that journaling is a good way to vent frustrations and can be tremendously therapeutic as well.

A MIXTURE OF APPREHENSION AND CONFUSION…
THEN RELIEF

Recalling my first session with Sandy in 1976, I'd have to characterize it as disjointed, something I am certain is true for anyone who, like me, is ready for therapy but has never been to a therapist. While I was eager to go, I didn't have any idea what to expect. I did have conventional expectations running through my mind though…would Dr. Macdonald be like that? In my mind a therapist was a stern man in a dark suit sitting rather stuffily in a sterile-looking office. He might look like Freud, writing on a pad of paper while listening to his couch-lying patient. While I certainly did not anticipate such a stereotypic scene, I wasn't sure what to expect. I was definitely curious about his office and about him, though, and wondered how we would begin.

Well, Sandy certainly didn't look stern. I immediately picked up on that because he was smiling. No recliner, but three easy chairs, a bookcase and small tables. The casual sweater he was wearing replaced the imagined dark suit. So much for expectations…

"Tell me a little about yourself," Sandy had said.

I began…immediate family, from Colorado, Gary at the university, etc.

Veering off course a little, I told him that I was acquainted with his wife, Betty, who was a psychologist in the State College School District. I often substituted at the schools where Betty was assigned and had gotten to know her over lunch. Then Sandy and I talked a bit about my teaching background.

Finally we got into the reasons I was there...my lack of confidence, feelings of unhappiness, at loose ends, depressed and restless. I told him about the day in the den, about Dr. Carney and about the fact that he, Sandy, was respected in town and highly recommended.

(My first choice would actually have been one of Sandy's partners because I had heard more about him, but our children were in preschool together and we had seen him and his wife socially. I felt our relationship should remain strictly social even though I now know that this was naïve of me.) Like I said, though, mental problems were not something you were proud of having. The fewer friends and acquaintances that knew of my state of mind, the better. Going to someone I had never met assured that this would be the case. In retrospect, the fact that I decided not to go to Sandy's partner was a very good decision since it led me to Sandy.

A GOOD START...

At Sandy's office we discussed the prescription I was taking. He explained the side effects and answered questions that I had. He told me that the amount I needed would be determined by how well I was feeling and that it would be slowly increased or decreased until the optimum dosage was reached.

After our initial session, subsequent meetings were easier because we had gotten beyond the starting point. It was easier for both of us, him to ask probing questions and me to feel like I had somewhat of a handle on what we were discussing. He would inquire about my journal writing. Was I writing every day? What was I writing? How was I feeling? Was it getting easier to cope? Was I tolerating the medication well?

"Give me examples of times when you feel lack of confidence? Do you feel that way at home sometimes?" Sandy would ask.

I would tell him about situations where feelings of inferiority might come up, or times when I would have difficulty concentrating or talking intelligently. All this time, Sandy would sit there patiently, smiling slightly, taking notes and making me feel comfortable.

TWO FOR THE PRICE OF ONE

After I told Gary that I was seeing a therapist, we both attended the next couple of sessions. Gary intently listened as Sandy explained this illness and all that its victims experience. Sandy made it clear that while this may well be the only bout I would suffer, chances are that it would not. Upon his recommendation we purchased two copies of the first book he asked us to read, *I'm OK, You're OK* by Thomas M. Harris, M.D. The book had been recently released, and Harris' theories of human behavior, based on the transactional analysis developed by Eric Berne in the fifties, advocated that we are responsible for what happens in the future. He maintains that our individual personalities are composed of parent, adult and child (P-A-C) and that our relationship with others is dependent upon which aspect of our personality we use when interacting. A mature individual sees the world as I'm OK, You're OK.

We left feeling very hopeful; we anticipated that reading the book might give us a picture not only of depression, but also of what we could do to hasten my recovery.

We found *I'm OK, You're OK* to be extremely informative, and, in fact, got into "critiquing" our individual behavior, in general, and toward one another in particular. It quickly became apparent that, when depressed, the adult dominates...lots of "I "should" have, Why "didn't" I and I "ought" to". Parent language was rampant, particularly within my thinking. When I was depressed, I was always "inside my mind"...questioning, pondering, regretting...so I had an abundance of situations that served as examples of my P-A-C communication, not only to myself but in the endless conversations I had with Gary.

Similarly, Gary's interaction with me was mainly coming from the parent... Here's what you "should" do. You "ought" to consider trying to jog? "Don't" stay home; rather, run an errand or two or meet me for lunch." To be fair, I needed a parent because I had become a helpless child who was solely dependent upon him. But, there was also adult coming from him as well.

"What do you plan to do this afternoon? You seem to be doing quite well."

Noticeably absent from a large percentage of my thoughts and our conversations was the child...no laughter, no spontaneous activities just for fun. There can't be, not when depression is severe. Life is anything but fun, laughter is but a memory and the thought of pleasurable activities is ludicrous.

Laughter wasn't entirely lacking in my life because when I was with my children, I was happy. They truly brought me joy. It was the Old Ann who was with them as we read, played and laughed together. It was, I now realize, part of the disassociating from who I had become that allowed the emergence of who I used to be. I shut out my nemesis, the love for my children being too strong. This would not prove to be the case years later with my grandson, Max, but at that time my depression had relentlessly deepened. I have learned that just when you believe that the depths of despair could not be more severe, you painfully discover that they can be.

* * *

Gary's attendance at initial sessions each time I would find myself in the depths of darkness was tremendously helpful. Lack of concentration and inability to adequately express myself made it essential that someone accompany me. Given the fact that increased depression means a decrease of concentration and rationality, it was important that another set of ears be there (along with the rest of the body, of course).

Gary was able to hear all that was meant for me to hear, to help me more fully explain all that was happening to me. He was able to listen to what Sandy was telling me. Because he was with me, this gave two of us the opportunity to discuss what was said and what Sandy had suggested that I do to help myself. Sometimes it involved a dosage change in my medication or responses to my many questions. Gary's being there was a great comfort, not only to me, but to him as well.

But while I loved having him at my sessions when I was really down, I got to a point when I began to resent him being there. I guess that meant I was getting better. But I also was a little argumentative. After one doctor's visit, I grumbled to Gary, "Enough said. This is my session. Remember, I'm the one who is depressed."

He would take my complaints in stride and allow me to use more of the time for myself. Verbosity is one of Gary's qualities. Clearly, what he says is interesting, informative and, often, humorous. But not on *my* time.

QUITTING THE SESSIONS

After session number five, we made a three-way decision to terminate my sessions. I was doing much better. I was reading and writing in my journal. Gary was empathetic and supportive. The cards were all in my favor, and I am certain that all of this made Sandy's recommendation much easier.

Earlier Dr. Carney had told me that it was likely that the illness would be a part of my life from time to time. I believed him, but given that we often put too much confidence in the hope that we feel, it had been my expectation that it would be years before another bout would enter my life. I had shoved the thought to the back of my mind. But, after having to return to Sandy's care that second time—only eighteen months later—I promised myself that I would never again quit going to therapy. I have kept that promise.

Once again, my medication was reviewed and adjusted. That became a key strategy for me. Each time I thought about changing medication because it didn't seem to be working, I would fully discuss the change with Sandy. I have always had these conversations with my Colorado therapists. While discussing the options, bits of hope would filter into my thinking and I would become optimistic that my symptoms would subside. Having a professional to talk with about this is much better than simply reading about it. This is another positive that comes from therapy sessions.

WITNESSING THE BENEFITS OF THERAPY FIRSTHAND

Since my father had suffered from severe depression in the midst of World War II, I knew that the fact that he had psychiatric help was a major reason for his recovery. He had received therapy when he was first taken to a military hospital in Utah and, again, when we lived on the grounds of the Colorado State Hospital upon his return to our hometown of Pueblo.

I know that he recognized the value of psychiatric help; if he had lived at the mental hospital for a year, he must have believed that it was important to his recovery. In looking back at all of it, I know that he would have been neither the confident person nor the competent physician that he was for all those years following his recovery had he not received psychiatric support. I can't imagine those who have faced horror in combat not seeking therapy, but many do not. And, many suffer the effects of all of it the rest of their lives.

I had no hesitation in getting psychiatric help once it finally occurred to me that that was what I needed. I have always had excellent rapport with both psychologists and psychiatrists, and have found that how each relates to their patients depends upon the expertise of each rather than the degree on the office wall. When you think of therapy, you might assume that it would be a psychiatrist that would be providing it, but I have had several excellent therapists that were either psychologists or nurse practitioners in addition to the two psychiatrists whose help I sought.

COMMITMENT, TIME AND PATIENCE PAYS OFF

It pays to be very careful in selecting a therapist, asking for references from numerous doctors and/or individuals who have either been or currently are in therapy. For this reason, I have had excellent medical assistance while combating this illness.

Therapy is not something that you just sit back and let happen. I have heard people comment that they tried it, but that "it didn't work for me." A common criticism is that the therapist wouldn't give them definitive answers. Another comment I would hear is that after several sessions, they quit going because they didn't feel any better. Still others sit in one session after another and do nothing in between sessions to help themselves.

Therapy takes time and patience. It consists of verbal exchanges between patient and therapist rather than sitting and listening to what the therapist has to say. Don't count on a good therapist to say much, actually, because you are expected to do the talking. Therapy involves reflective listening, digging deep, and discussing options. And, most importantly, therapy is work...a *lot* of work.

If you are to gain from your therapeutic sessions, it is important that you hold nothing back when discussing your thoughts and fears. Honesty is crucial. If you are going to be truthful, you really have to believe that all that is discussed is strictly confidential. Therapists make this clear during the initial meeting, but this is something that you have to firmly believe. Without this trust, honesty is not possible; and, without honesty, your recovery is hampered from the very beginning.

YOU HAVE TO DO MORE THAN OPEN THE BOOKS

After Gary and I read all the suggested books, we discussed them with the Sandy as we attempted to understand this complex illness that appeared out of the blue. We were willing to do whatever it took to put our lives back together again.

Many people find doctors intimidating. I have had the advantage of being raised in a family of medical doctors since both my grandfather and my father were physicians. My confidence is apparent upon meeting someone new and continues through our professional relationship. If you don't have confidence, I suggest you work hard to muster up all that you can. It's crucial that you ask questions, understand what is being said and follow through with any concerns you have by doing your own research. It's helpful to write questions down before you go and have a notebook with you to write in. The lack of concentration and the "fog" that surrounds all thinking is a detriment. Taking a family member along is always a good idea.

* * *

I have never understood people who just sit back and expect depression to pass. They want instant answers, are not willing to wait for progress and then blame their therapist. They are convinced that therapy does not work. I know differently. If you have a reputable therapist, therapy will be effective, but only if you do the work. Why would you not want to help yourself...and put in the effort to get better?

CHAPTER 22:
Medication, Part I

JOURNAL ENTRY
State College, Pennsylvania November 23, 1985

I awoke with my body tingling with anxiety; thoughts raced about past regrets and apprehensions about future events. Dr. Nabavi, the psychiatrist recommended by Sandy, has suggested that I try lithium.

This may help the mood swings. Research indicates that, while lithium must be carefully monitored, it can be quite effective.

M edication and therapy go hand in hand (my mantra). This is the opinion of most medical experts, and is unquestionably true in my case. Throughout the book, I have demonstrated the value of each. This chapter brings to light more of the issues about my taking medication. In the following chapter I provide a list of the drugs I took over the years and their side effects.

I was always receptive to both components of my recovery process — medication and therapy — but at the beginning I'd had no idea how long it was going to take to realize any effects. The big unknown. This was especially true for the medications. At least with therapy, I could leave the doctor's office and feel some relief and comfort, but the drugs might take weeks before I noticed a difference at all. I naively thought that with prescription in hand and a call to a psychologist I would return to my former self within a few months time...happily going about my life, maintained on this wonder drug.

LIFELINE #1

I first started taking medication for depression in the fall of 1976. Antidepressants in the seventies were quite different than they are today. Side effects were often more serious. Fewer options were available, so if one drug was not useful, alternatives were limited. I have changed medications several times. Sometimes the ineffectiveness of a particular drug warranted a change; other times, newer drugs came on the market that were considered superior to what I was taking. Newer drugs are often more refined and consequently have fewer serious side effects.

I am convinced that, in my particular case, antidepressants are necessary. This may not be true for others, but it is for me. From time to time, I hear about victims of suicide who had gone off their medication...and I can't imagine. I can't imagine.

But each individual has different needs, different degrees of this illness and different beliefs of what they feel is best for them. It's not for me to criticize the choices others have made. I expect the same from others. You have to do what is best for you. I know that medication is necessary if I am to function well. I *know* because there have been times that I have regretted my decision to go without medication, thinking that I no longer needed it. I have learned hard lessons.

* * *

Let's address degrees and types of depression. Many people espouse their belief that you can recover from depression sans medication. In many instances, this is true. If your depression is mild or can be linked to external misfortunes such as a family death or loss of a job, time will take care of the pain.

Chemical imbalance, however, is far different, and is the reason that I have endured this affliction for so many years. Certainly, external events can trigger it, but the underlying cause of *my* depression is chemical balance. Just as painkillers ease pain, blood pressure medication lowers blood pressure or thyroid medication creates normal ranges within our body, antidepressant medication balances our brain chemistry.

I am aware that there are those who adamantly believe that medication is not necessary, and I am in agreement that antidepressants are often prescribed too quickly. When Prozac arrived on the scene, I know that this was often the case. People were popping them left and right, prescription pads were used at record rates. Now, though, I don't think writing prescriptions is as prevalent, but I have no concrete evidence of this.

I do not pretend to be a medical expert. I know that I am not capable of telling anyone what he or she should or should not do. On occasion I have suggested to others that they may want to discuss their depression/anxiety with their physician because medication can get you "over the hump" so that you will once again be able to function. Catastrophic events such as divorce often create downward spins, severe anxiety and that "out of control" panic. Since there is help available, *I* (and I emphasis *I*) firmly believe that you should take advantage of it. Why continue to be close to non-functional? Yet many do choose that course.

Positive thinking and other cognitive therapy strategies can be of tremendous help, as can religion/meditation/yoga or tai chi, if you are so inclined. I have certainly found them to be.

BEING YOUR OWN MEDICATION "EXPERT"

It behooves you to always be open to making medication changes when it is likely that a new drug may be more effective. That is a good rule of thumb, and one I usually followed, but at times I have decided to stay with the medication I was currently taking rather than switch. Whether I remained on my current medication or opted for change, I was always very involved in the decision because I am fully aware...I cannot stress this enough... that no one is more interested in my well being than I am.

* * *

Unlike psychiatrists, psychologists cannot prescribe medication. Their role is more of coordinator with family physicians to recommend appropriate antidepressants for a patient. A good mental health provider keeps communication open with the family physician of his or her patients. It is important to find a provider who will do this as part of your care.

I have made it a practice to always read the literature on recommended drugs before I agreed to take them. Their side effects and any negative research findings were two of the primary considerations when making my decision to say yes to them. Once the Internet became available, my research was more systematic. As time went on, selected websites made it possible to do extensive comparing, obtain more professional opinions and understand research options more thoroughly. It is crucial, though, that credible websites are consulted (there are many medical websites, but not all are trustworthy). The National Institute of Health, Medline Plus and Web MD are three I found authoritative. The Internet also allows me to review actual research findings of scientists, medical, and pharmacological researchers in the fields of depression and/or medication.

A typical example of how I used the Internet was when I stopped taking a drug called Xanax and suspected that I was experiencing withdrawal symptoms. After consulting several websites, I realized that, indeed, I was. The information corresponded with my symptoms at that time: insomnia, nervousness and stomach cramps. Discovering that the cause was the Xanax withdrawal was a great relief, because I was convinced that something else, unrelated to my mental problems, was wrong.

Throughout the years I have taken a variety of antidepressants/mood stabilizers/anxiety drugs. I hadn't realized that I would need to make so many changes after I had finally adjusted to one. Sometimes the effectiveness lessens, but because new drugs are often being approved, there are always other options.

JOURNAL ENTRY
Oxford, Mississippi May 8, 2000

Another bad night—extreme stomach disorder symptoms. I know now why this is happening. Quitting Xanax has resulted in withdrawal symptoms (anxiety, vision deficiency, headache and the dizziness and several others that have now manifested themselves are all withdrawal symptoms of this drug).

I talked with Mary Chapman at length about my assessment as well as about her suggestions regarding medication. I am sticking with Serzone because its effectiveness was reduced when combined with the Xanax I was taking. I will up Serzone by 100 mg.

It's been rough, but it will pass...just hard to endure until it does.

THE OH-SO-LONG WAITING PERIOD

Waiting for a medication to take effect was the most difficult part. The time period always seemed much longer than it actually was, and knowing that it could prove to be ineffective added even more unpredictability to the equation. I knew I had to be patient, but at least I always had the slightest bit of hope that the medication *might* work. And then, once I began feeling somewhat better, the dosages would be adjusted until the proper amount was determined (a little higher or lower). It was always a slow process.

With the exception of Prozac and later Celexa, I have tolerated all recommendations and have found them to be quite useful in appeasing my depression. I have never found side effects to be a major problem. Putting up with constipation, diarrhea, muscle ache, edginess and/or fatigue and drowsiness are nothing compared to what I would experience *without* the medication. In most cases, the side effects would abate considerably and my life would be good... until the next time.

As side effects go, I didn't worry about most. Drug manufacturers list everything and anything that one might experience while on the drug. They do this for liability purposes, i.e., to cover their butts! I only considered the more common ones.

A good example is when I changed from Tegretol to Lamictal in 2001. Dr. Bell and I went over several options before I decided on Lamictal. He immediately ruled out a couple because he knew their side effects were things I was not willing to tolerate. They were the dreaded two...hair loss and weight gain.

"I think Lamictal might be a good possibility," Dr. Bell suggested.

"What are the side effects?"

"We'll start with the worst...you could die," he said with a smile on his face. (I need to tell you that by this time our relationship was a comfortable one, as this remark demonstrates.)

"Well, at least I wouldn't be in any pain for long."

We selected Lamictal, keeping a watchful eye for the "severe rash" that would lead to death if I continued to take it.

The drugs I have taken in the past for the most part include Triavil, Zoloft, Lithium, Xanax, Prozac, Serzone, Celexa, Ambien, Tegretol, Effexor XR and Lamictal. See the next chapter for details. I have gone back to some of them when new ones were less tolerable so I have had more medication changes than I have had different kinds of medication.

After doing all this research over the years, I felt like I was becoming the master of my disease. I knew the right questions to ask about every new potential drug that came along. I kept track of my illness and my medications in my journal so I had a complete history.

This was happening to *me*, so I wanted to have the upper hand. While you can't control your depression, you *can* control how you attempt to combat it. Control...make sure you always have it.

QUESTIONING, QUESTIONING, QUESTIONING

Have you ever read a "patient package insert"? They are the little "reports" that come with your prescription drugs that list, in very small print, all the drug interactions, contraindications, symptoms, etc., etc., I read all of them. I also continue to research the Internet, asking such questions as: What are the advantages/disadvantages of each? What are the side effects? Would any of those I am considering negatively interact with other medications I might be taking? (Asking a pharmacist also is a good idea.)

An important word about pharmacists...I have found them to be an invaluable resource. Your physicians may be familiar with antidepressant medications, but very few of them are experts. (My Denver psychiatrist, Dr. Jon Bell happens to be.) Pharmacists, on the other hand, are current on the drugs that they dispense. Competent ones (make sure you consult only competent ones) look for any interaction your prescribed drugs may have with one another. It was a pharmacist in Oxford, Mississippi who alerted me to the fact that it was the Xanax interaction with Serzone that was depleting the strength of the Serzone. Had he not informed me of this fact, I would never have known. A reputable Internet site confirmed this...I then let my doctor in on this finding! See why you need to be "in control?"

I have been fortunate to have my "personal pharmacist" with whom I consult any time of day. My brother-in-law, Dave Kochenberger, heads the pharmacy at the Colorado State Hospital, a mental hospital. It is, therefore, imperative that he is current on the drugs that become available as well as the ones that have proven effectiveness as well as the many side effects of each. Because he has access to the most current information, coupled with the fact that he is an excellent pharmacist, I know that I am able to solicit his expert opinion. Incidentally, he always concurs with Dr. Bell's recommendations and this reinforces my trust in Dr. Bell.

The topic of side effects alone could fill a book. With antidepressants and mood-altering drugs, there are many, some more severe than others, but this depends on each individual's tolerance of each particular drug. Just because there are ten side effects listed for a drug doesn't mean you will experience all ten.

When deciding on a medication choice, I discuss it with the medical expert I am currently seeing. We consult together and go over the percentage of people who experience each of the common side effects. I consider only the ones that are most likely to appear, although I am certainly aware of those that are less common or rare. I wholeheartedly recommend that you stay involved with treatment decisions. Never agree to take something that you have not researched, discussed at length or do not feel comfortable taking.

ADDICTION

I am an incredibly disciplined person, but I often have to work very hard at not becoming addicted to something when I am depressed. You just want so badly to feel better and you know that popping a pill will result in a change of mood. I know I kept Xanax in my cabinet far longer than I needed to, however, which is a good indication that I was psychologically dependent on it. I often rejected the temptation to ingest one of those teeny white pills...for me it was a comfort just knowing that it was there. I find it amazing that I am able to be so strong in times of such lures, but I am somehow able to monitor my prescriptions, just as I have always carefully monitored any drinking of alcoholic beverages.

It is important for me to make certain that there is no pattern to my consumption of wine; I also allow myself only one glass. Knowing that I *have* to enjoy that one glass every night would make me an alcoholic, since it is the dependency rather than the quantity, I never indulge each night. My mother became an alcoholic after the sudden death of my father when, at age 44, she found herself sole parent of the six of us. I thought she was old at that time since I was only eighteen, but as I grew older I came to realize how very difficult this must have been for her. Some of her ancestors, as well as several on my father's side of the family, had drinking problems. Genetically, just as is true with depression, there is a tendency to inherit the same addiction. This is something that I firmly believe everyone who had such a history needs to keep in mind.

SNAPSHOT
Denver, Colorado   September 1992

Last year was long and painful. I knew that I needed to try another anti-depressant, but I should have tried a new one earlier in the summer. I am grateful for my doctor because he understands my need for medication and is familiar with the various choices.

The school year has just begun and the Prozac is not working. It sounded like a good choice because it has been so effective for so many people, but it isn't working for me.

I constantly feel "wired," I have difficulty sleeping and the depression remains.

Waiting in the faculty lounge for my doctor's nurse to return my call, I know that something has to be done. I cannot go through another year like last year.

The journal entries I read last night were verification of the ineffectiveness of the Prozac I have been taking. Being depressed for 18 of the 21 days that I have been on this drug was certainly an indication. Waking early, along with anxiety and feelings of despondency do not ensure a good school day. It may be that these symptoms will subside and I will adjust to this drug, but I am not able to wait this out and competently teach a room filled with second graders.

I have to go back on the amitriptyline (Triavil). Even though it is not one of the newer drugs, I know that I am not depressed while taking it. This is not the time to fool around with an adjustment period of a new medication. What if, like the Prozac, an alternative doesn't work? Then I have to try yet another.

> The side effects I had while on the amitriptyline were nothing compared to what I am now experiencing. I will continue with it for the remainder of the year and will consider a change during the summer. Perhaps I will go back on Zoloft.
>
> The nurse agrees with my assessment and will have the doctor prescribe amitriptyline. I am so relieved. I think I will stop at the club on the way home…nothing like exercise for the mood. This, along with the decision to change the negative things in my life and hope that something else will lead to a better tomorrow.

Living with depression is ongoing; it is a constant case of keeping up with medication research. Questions, searching websites for information and consulting with my psychologist or psychiatrist is necessary if I am to do the best for myself. Not an easy thing when in the midst of depression, but this is part of the way I have lived my life.

RECOVERING WITHOUT MEDICATION

There are those who, for religious reasons, never take medication; other people see doing so as a sign of weakness. They believe they can "handle it" and view "pill-popping" as a crutch. Many people believe that those who experience depression need to let it run its course, to just get over it rather than take medication. An example of this view is actor Tom Cruise's public criticism in 2006 of Brook Shield's decision to take medication for postpartum depression. Obviously Mr. Cruise has never suffered the ravages of this debilitating illness. The criticism of him by millions who know that because of modern medicine they are now able to live normal lives was warranted. More people are speaking out about the importance of seeking help; and this, I believe, is the reason so many are now feeling positive about obtaining the assistance that they need.

Mr. Cruise eventually apologized to Brook Shields. Could it have had anything to do with living with actress Katie Holmes and witnessing her recovery following the birth of their baby?

Well, call me weak and hand me that crutch. I emphatically believe that agreeing to medication is *not* a weakness but a way to correct the chemical imbalance that is the cause of this illness.

THE THINGS THAT MEDICATION CAN'T FIX

I was in for a rude awakening. Not only did it take much longer for the medication to work, but once the bout of depression was over, I was left with the remnants of what the illness had done to my self-esteem and confidence. Drugs couldn't fix that.

It is not surprising that this illness strips you of self-confidence. When you are in the midst of it, lack of concentration is a big part of all that you are not able to do. I guess we fail to think about how much we rely on being able to concentrate. We concentrate on what we want to say, what we are about to say once others are finished talking and what we do say as we speak. Once all of that is absorbed, we may want to respond once again. It would be impossible to do any of this if we were not able to focus. Taking this further, we focus when we drive places, when we read the newspaper, listen to the news. We concentrate as we go about our daily tasks...counting out money, completing transactions in stores, attending meetings or functions. Everything we do requires our full attention, or at least our partial attention (ask those who drive while talking on cell phones!).

It only stands to reason, then, that as we begin to recover, we look for improvement in all areas of our lives...our relationships with others, our ability to complete tasks and our ability to laugh and love once again. This is probably why it is called the "recovery process." It *is* a process...a long process.

Depression saps you of your energy. When deeply affected, it is an effort to get dressed or walk to the mailbox. You find yourself procrastinating about miniscule chores simply because it would be too overwhelming to complete them.

And then there are the people who were the recipients of your ineptitudes. How can you face them after you have made no sense in front of them on former occasions? What must they think of you? This is terribly difficult. You have to "begin anew" with such people, proving your competence once again.

There were some situations that I handled poorly, only to have to work hard to rebuild my confidence so that I could demonstrate my worth to those who had witnessed my behavior. This was not easy because there was pressure to do more than perform well...I had to rebuild *their* confidence in *me* at the same time I was rebuilding confidence in *myself*. In addition to being difficult, it is not accomplished quickly. It takes time but, until that time came, I was satisfied with myself because I knew the reasons behind my incompetence and I knew that it *would* take time. I have always done the best I am able to do, and knowing that is a huge comfort to me.

I remember a situation when I was a researcher/writer at the Penn State Foundation (known as The Office of Gifts and Endowments at that time.) This was back in the early eighties when I was hired as the sole researcher to gather information on perspective Penn State donors. I would write up reports on foundations, corporations and individuals, submit the reports to our foundation officers who would then have pertinent information before they would meet with representatives of the targeted monies sources.

Our staff was attending the regular meeting chaired by Charlie Lupton who was head of Gifts and Endowments. He singled me out during that meeting, complimenting me on the quality of my work. Since my mental stability was rather shaky at that time, I sat there wondering how I was able to fool so many people. Why would someone praise my capabilities when I was convinced that I had none?

The hours I spent at Pattee Library allowed me an escape from the darkness I would reenter each time I walked out. I submerged myself in the resource books, loving the challenge of gathering pertinent information to use in my reports. The solitude I so sought was there. I worked alone. I was able to be me in a world I loved...that of books, learning and writing.

Back at my office, typing my findings was less comfortable because other people surrounded me. My phone might ring; someone might stop by with a request. All of this was confusing, and confusion was not conducive to the manner in which I functioned best. But I was determined to do the best I could. I told myself that constantly each and every day..."Do the best you can. Do the best you can. Do the best you can"...because that was the most I could do. And going to bed each night, knowing that I gave everything I was able to give that day, was something of which I was very proud, and I am certain that I slept better because of it.

All of this reaped benefits because once my depression vanished, my confidence was even higher than it would have been had I not worked so terribly hard to do well. I was able to see things more clearly, living in the reality in which those who are mentally healthy live. I was able to see that the incompetence I was convinced I had had not been there at all. I was able to recognize my work for the quality work it really was...

CHAPTER 23:
Medication II

Listed below are the different medications I have used to treat my depression along with the side effects and some discussion of each. This list provides an illustration of all the data that goes into my thought processes as I have selected one drug over the other. Rather than include less common and rare side effects of each, I have listed only the common side effects because these are more likely to manifest themselves.

I have listed the medications *in the order in which they were prescribed throughout the years*. Keep in mind that drugs have different effects on each individual. While listed side effects may include both insomnia and drowsiness, one person may experience agitation while another might experience exhaustion.

While this chapter may seem too lengthy for some who read this book, I made the choice to keep it the way I have written it. Finding the right medication, time after time again, is, in itself a very lengthy process. By listing the many side effects one might incur, the point is explicitly made that making that decision to try a particular medication is much more of a thought process than one might assume.

1. **Triavil** was the first antidepressant I took. It is part of a group of drugs that fall under the category of amitriptyline. It was back in the mid-seventies, when I first was diagnosed, that I took this medication. In later years drugs had fewer side effects and were much more effective in reducing symptoms of the illness. At the time, though, Triavil seemed to help quite a bit.

   Caution: Side effects include constipation, extreme drowsiness, severe muscle stiffness; fever; weakness; dryness of the mouth; dizziness if getting up quickly; blurred vision; difficulty speaking or swallowing; inability to move eyes; lip smacking or puckering; loss of bladder control; mask-like face; muscle spasms; nervousness; restlessness; desire to keep moving; puffing of cheeks; rapid or fine worm-like movement of tongue; shuffling walk; stiffness of arms and legs; trembling and shaking of fingers and hands; tic-like or twitching movements; twisting movements of body; uncontrolled chewing movements; uncontrolled movement of arms and legs; weakness of arms and legs

Although I felt rather dizzy initially on Triavil, I was fortunate because the only inconveniences I consistently experienced were constipation, extreme drowsiness and dryness of mouth. These are things that can easily be tolerated and are definitely more desirable than being depressed. In particular, the extreme drowsiness was a welcome relief that enabled me to fall asleep quickly, something that was often difficult for me to do otherwise.

Like any drug, it is safer to work up to your maximum dosage. When I first went back on Triavil after being off it for years, I took the dosage I had taken prior to going off the drug and I was zonked. This was in the late nineties when the school year was beginning and I needed to take something that I knew had been effective. I should have known better. I was quickly reminded of the reason for working up to your optimum dosage rather than taking up where you left off. I was feeling far beyond tired. I felt drugged (you are, of course, but I mean it in the sense of feeling heavy and experiencing inability to move freely).

2. **Xanax**, an anti-anxiety medication, is one of the tiniest pills I have ever seen. Despite its size, it is a classic example of a big thing coming in a small package.

JOURNAL ENTRY
State College, Pennsylvania August 14, 1985

Depressed when I awoke at 5:45 (early awakening), took a Xanax at 6:00 and felt better soon after 8:00. I like the office atmosphere at Alumni, but I feel paranoid about the Office of University Development. Saw Sandy...will begin dream analysis and intensive therapy. Interesting!

Felt great during and after a two-hour tennis match with Betz Hanley.

Anxiety is a huge ongoing part of my depression and extremely difficult to tolerate. I would feel "wired," shaky and unsteady. It was difficult to sit still, and I always had to be moving. My skin, particularly arms and neck, felt clammy and cold. During one three-month episode when we first moved from Pennsylvania to Colorado (1984), my arms and neck tingled and it felt as if my skin was "lifting upwards." The obsession of worry and regret accompanied all of these symptoms causing the anxiety to heighten. Because that had never happened before (oh boy, a new symptom!), it made me more anxious. Why was this happening? Maybe something is physically wrong. My skin feels so weird! When we lived in Denver in 1984-1985, it was Dr. Feiger who was providing psychiatric care and prescribing my medication. He assured me that it was stress that was causing severe anxiety. This was a different side of anxiety and each time a new symptom is felt, you are convinced that there must be something else physically wrong. Just when you think you are able to predict what might happen to you, this illness reminds you of its unpredictability.

These are some of the many symptoms people feel when they are anxious. It is a terrible feeling, so when things became unbearable, I would often take a Xanax pill. I was careful not to do so on a regular basis, though, because this drug is known for being highly addictive. Like Valium, it is a "take as needed" drug rather than one taken on a consistent basis.

Since I was cognizant of becoming addicted, I only took the small pill when my anxiety level was so high that I could no longer endure its symptoms. Just as I did when I was suicidal, I played mind games with myself. The comfort of knowing that the prescription sat in my medicine cabinet was enough to alleviate some of the anxiety...just enough to convince me that I really didn't have to take a Xanax at that time. But I knew that I *could* take one if things got really bad. Many times, half a pill would do the job. It works quickly and is very efficient.

I have a good friend who had to check into a hospital because he was addicted to the Xanax he was taking for severe back pain. Another friend had to taper off by cutting the pill in fourths and taking one-fourth less a week at a time. I'm glad I didn't have to reduce my dosage more than going down to half a pill because its hard for me to imagine cutting the tiniest pill I have ever taken (or seen) into four parts!

Caution: Side effects include clumsiness or unsteadiness; dizziness; drowsiness; slurred speech, irritability; difficulty sleeping; lightheadedness; talkativeness; weight changes; difficulty urinating; changes in appetite; addiction; difficulty falling asleep; sore throat; changes in sex drive; excessive sweating

3. **Zoloft** was a medication I took for a couple of years. It worked well for me but I had no sex drive, so I decided to switch because of that reason. Not having a sex drive was no problem for me because when I'm depressed sex is the last thing on my mind. However, since I live with the man to whom I credit saving my life by guiding me through this depression, I owed it to him to attempt to muster up some sort of spark. I certainly could have "faked it," but, as most will agree, its more fun when there is desire behind this activity, so I discussed alternatives with my Pueblo physician, Jim Sternholjm. In retrospect, I regretted doing this because the alternative choice he suggested was not effective and it took some time to stabilize my medication. Lack of sex drive is much easier to tolerate than are the symptoms of depression.

   Caution: Side effects of Zoloft include upset stomach; diarrhea; constipation; nervousness; shaking hands that you cannot control. vomiting; dry mouth; gas or bloating; loss of appetite; weight changes; drowsiness; dizziness; excessive fatigue; pain, burning or tingling of the hands or feet; excitement

4. **Lithium**, used to treat and prevent manic episodes (frenzy, abnormally excited mood) in people with bipolar disorders, works by decreasing abnormal activity in the brain. I was reluctant to take this drug after it was initially recommended because its therapeutic range is very narrow and must be consistently monitored with blood level testing. If not properly monitored, it is either ineffective or results in side effects that are quite troublesome. After the second doctor recommended it, however, I decided that I would give it a try.

   Caution: Side effects include restlessness; fine hand movements that are difficult to control; loss of appetite; stomach pain; gas; indigestion; weight gain or loss; dry mouth; excessive saliva; tongue pain; changes in ability to taste food; swollen lips; acne; hair loss; unusual discomfort in cold temperatures; constipation; depression; joint or muscle pain; thin fingernails, brittle hair

These are undesirable enough...not able to manage fine hand control? Tongue pain? Swollen lips and hair loss? Sounds like great fun!

But more serious side effects to lithium include body tremors; seizures; loss of coordination; excessive thirst; giddiness; ringing in ears; jerky, slow movements; slurred speech; hallucinations; headache; pounding noises inside of head; changes in vision. These are the ones about which you need to worry.

For me, despite blood level testing, this medication caused my thyroid to completely shut down, something that was discovered only three months after starting the drug. I was excessively tired, something I initially attributed to the rush of the holiday season, along with my full-time teaching job. My family doctor, Jim Sternholjm, a highly respected physician in Pueblo, was very surprised and remarked that he had never had a patient whose body had reacted that quickly. I went off the drug and was prescribed another, as well as thyroid pills.

I was relieved to know that the lithium was the cause of the fatigue rather than old age! I was under the mistaken impression that I would never again have the vigor that I had so valued.

5. **Prozac**, touted as the "wonder drug" for everybody, was not wonderful for me. You were considered one of the "in crowd" if you were on Prozac. It almost became rather cultish, so much so that those who took it flaunted it as a status symbol. If I correctly remember, Prozac was big during the late eighties and early nineties. It was the drug of choice for the stars, part of the script in many movies and the topic of conversation among the general public.

When my family doctor recommended it to me, I thought, "Why not?" After all, it seemed to be working miracles for millions, and I certainly could use something that would "miraculously" cure my dark mood. Alas, it was not to be.

Caution: Side effects include decreased sex drive; inability to sit still; restlessness; skin rash; hives; itching; decreased appetite; diarrhea; excessive sweating; nausea; weakness; trembling; tiredness

I was on this drug for twenty-one days and experienced severe insomnia and nausea, was extremely agitated and jittery and, most unfortunately, exceedingly depressed. Yikes, it was doing the opposite for me! I had always been able to wait out side effects when changing medication. Even though the symptoms can be extremely uncomfortable, I know they will eventually dissipate—at least most will. It takes anywhere from three to six weeks to adjust to a new drug. But the side effects I experienced with Prozac were intolerable. Managing this illness is difficult enough, but even more so with only an hour or two of sleep each night. I was not going to wait it out this time and went off it immediately!

6. **Serzone** was another antidepressant I have used, but I am not certain of the time period over which I took it. I know that it was the drug I was using when we moved to Mississippi in the summer of 1999. I decided to give something else a try when I began experiencing mild symptoms of depression during April and May of the following spring.

   Caution: Side effects of Serzone include blurred vision; unsteadiness; light headedness or fainting; ringing in the ears; skin rash or itching; agitation; abnormal dreams; confusion; constipation or diarrhea; drowsiness; headache; increased appetite; cough; memory problems; nausea; prickly sensations; tremor; insomnia; and/or vomiting

7. **Celexa** was prescribed after Serzone, before my depression became severe while living in Oxford, Mississippi. My doctor thought that I would benefit by changing medications since I was beginning to experience depressive symptoms again. I was only too eager to change medication because I felt unstable mentally while on the Serzone. After researching several choices, I decided to go with Celexa.

   I'm not certain if it was the drug that caused me to plunge or if my depression just deepened, but the beginning of the worst episode I have ever endured started soon after I began that prescription. I can't remember how long I had been taking the daily dosage so it may well be that the medication had not even had time to take effect. I only know that I found myself in the middle of hell on earth and struggled desperately to survive for the next three months.

   Caution: Side effects of Celexa include decrease in sexual desire, agitation, blurred vision, confusion, frequency of urination or amount of urine produced; lack of emotion; loss of memory; skin rash or itching, trouble breathing

I was not able to tolerate Celexa and I believe it was completely ineffective in treating my depression. This suggests that since Celexa did nothing for me, it was as if I was not taking any medication at all. I had not gone without any medications since my early days of depression.

8. **Effexor XR** – the XR designates that this drug is time-released and this allows me to only take it once a day.

   Caution: Side effects of Effexor include upset stomach, drowsiness; weakness; insomnia; nightmares; dry mouth; skin more sensitive to sunlight; changes in appetite or weight; headache; constipation; difficulty urinating; frequent urination; blurred vision; changes in sex drive; excessive sweating; slow or slurred speech; shuffling walk; muscle spasms in jaw, neck or back; fever; difficulty breathing or swallowing; severe skin rash; yellowing of eyes or skin; irregular heartbeat

This drug may cause weight loss rather than weight gain. I am currently on Effexor and it is much better for sex drive, which is the reason I discontinued taking Zoloft. I remember that I had a bit of the slurred speech, but that went away. Other than that I have tolerated the drug very well.

9. **Tegretol** is not an antidepressant, although it is often prescribed to treat mania and bipolar conditions. It is in a classification of drugs called anti-convulsants and works by reducing abnormal excitement in the brain. It is referred to as a mood stabilizer, the effects of which "quiet" or stabilize the mind in the same way that it stabilizes physical seizures. It is often prescribed for physical conditions such as epilepsy.

   Caution: Side effects include drowsiness; dizziness; unsteadiness; upset stomach; vomiting; headache; anxiety; memory problems; diarrhea; constipation; heartburn; dry mouth and back pain

Dr. Bell prescribed this when I began taking Effexor. I took these two drugs daily and experienced no symptoms of depression, but within months I developed skin problems. Normally I easily bruised, even when I slightly bump an arm or leg, but not to this extent. There would be large black areas on my arms and the top of my hands that would appear and then fade. They would completely disappear, but another area would then blacken. It was unsightly more than anything else. Unusual bruising is considered a red flag but my blood level test indicated that I was tolerating the drug very well.

Another serious consideration when taking this medication is that it may decrease the number of blood cells produced by your body, which can, on rare occasions, cause serious and life-threatening health problems.

About four years after first taking Tegretol I began to experience fatigue that became quite severe. Thinking that my thyroid level may be off, I took yet another proactive stance and asked that a blood test be run. The evening of the day I had blood drawn, I received a call from the doctor who had read the report. He explained that their lab routinely alerted doctors immediately when major problems arise.

He asked me what medications I was on and when Tegretol came up, he told me to stop taking it immediately because it is a drug that can cause sodium levels to drop dangerously low. I was to make an appointment so that the levels could be read. I agreed to stop the medication, but knew that I had to consult with Dr. Bell. I called him that same evening and he concurred that this was exactly what I should do. At that time, we made an appointment to discuss an alternative mood stabilizer.

The lab results revealed a sodium level reading of 15, which is very low. Normal levels range between 35 and 40. Within about six weeks, my levels were very close to normal and I felt like a different person. My energy slowly returned until things were as they once were.

Dr. Bell and I discussed several alternatives. I opted for Lamictal and am currently taking this along with the Effexor, praying that they will always be effective.

10. **Lamictal** is an anticonvulsant medication rather than an antidepressant. Since Lamictal and other anticonvulsant drugs quiet physical spasms, mental health professionals were curious as to whether it would have the same effect on the brain. Why would this classification of drugs not quiet the mind as well as the body? It has proven to be very helpful in treating depression. I continue to take this with Effexor.

Caution: Side effects include drowsiness; trouble sleeping; dizziness; nausea; vomiting; loss of appetite; muscle aches; double vision; blurred vision; fatigue; weakness; shakiness; clumsiness, or <u>skin rash</u>.

Dr. Bell alerted me to this skin rash, telling me to immediately go off the drug if it should appear. I was so cognizant of this that when I developed "miniscule red spots on the inside of one arm," I quickly made an appointment with him.

"Nope," he said, "Not even close to the skin rash that would be a serious problem."

Whew!

I tolerate Lamictal well and have experienced no long-term side effects.

DEALING WITH SIDE EFFECTS

In reading over the many side effects of each drug I took to curb my depression, it quickly becomes apparent I spent a lot of time weighing the pros and cons. While I knew that I never wanted the side effects of hair loss or weight gain (either of which, I felt, would only *increase* my depression), side effects such as blurred vision, excessive sweating or breathing problems would not be easy to tolerate. But, you may only experience some of the symptoms—and most of what you might have to endure may only be temporary. Patience frequently pays off.

You must be flexible when on antidepressants because the body can become immune to medication once you have taken it for a long period of time. When this happens, alternatives need to be considered.

For me, the side effects were usually short-lived, but not always. An example was when I took Tegretol in 2001 and experienced drowsiness. I was instructed to take it before going to bed and the fact that I became extremely tired was a Godsend because I needed my sleep. There is nothing worse than insomnia so I gladly took my dosage each night.

While some people eat when depressed, I do the opposite. When depression hits hard, I cannot eat; I sometimes gag on food because my mouth gets so dry and I have no appetite whatsoever. Nothing sounds appealing. Not eating, coupled with the severe anxiety I have to endure, causes my weight to plunge at an alarming rate. It is as if pounds are shaken off in rapid succession with each tremor of anxiety. People who are unaware of my mental state remark that I look incredible; secretly I know that I would much rather not look so good and feel normal.

So, let's see...would I rather have uncontrollable shaking hands and excessive sweating or depression? How about falling and stumbling or double vision rather than being depressed? Naturally I would not want to experience any of these, but that's why we have options.

I am fortunate that I have had health insurance for my medication all these years. Even with that, however, the cost can be a hundred dollars each month. With rising co-pays, it adds up quickly. Many who do not have health insurance send to Canada for their medication. Drugs are perfectly safe when you use reputable pharmacies in that country; in fact, the sources used for many of what is prescribed are the same sources used by our pharmacies.

I did not have insurance for therapy for many years because it wasn't a part of many health plans. This fact assumed that mental instability wasn't considered an illness. I paid out of pocket, and was more than happy to do so. Some years later, my insurance paid 50% of each visit and, later still, it paid 80% so health providers now usually cover the many aspects of mental health. If you have to redo your budget, do what you can because it is essential (in my opinion) that you see a good therapist.

Will I have to take medication forever? I know from past experience that I will take medication the rest of my life. Many people are able to cease medication and continue on in life with no ill effects. This is often true when causes for depressive episodes are external, such as experiencing the death of a loved one, loss of a job or divorce. Depression can be an expected side effect and one for which temporary medication may help in the coping process. Check with your doctor about the length of time you will need to stay on your medication.

CHAPTER 24:
Little Things Can Make a Big Difference – Other Coping Techniques

I accumulated a variety of little techniques I could do that would ease some of my depression and anxiety. While each of these is important, its value at any given time could never be predicted, so I often incorporated them all. I often would do this in a panic...what might help? Maybe I should try this? I'm dying here!

Connecting with friends did me a world of good. Because I was able to often "disassociate" from my intruder, it was the Old Ann who met friends for tennis, coffee or lunch. I was in another world with them...talking about kids, goals or husbands. Laughing and planning for future excursions was wonderful.

The ability to switch from one personality to another is termed *disassociation*. I have always been able to do this unless my depression was too brutal. I knew that I was my old self around others, but I thought I was able to do so because of the fact that I wanted to hide my illness. It wasn't until thirty years later than I learned that there was an actual term for this.

In her book *Miss America By Day*, Marilyn Van Derbur lived her life by disassociating from her Night Child. It was the Night Child who was molested by her father from the age of five until she turned eighteen. (Van Derber, Marilyn. *Miss America By Day: Lessons Learned from Ultimate Betrayal and Unconditional Love*. Denver: Oak Hill Ridge Press, 2004.) Marilyn's father was a highly respected, well-to-do member of the Denver community, someone who years later many could never fathom doing the things his daughter said he did. But after she was put to bed, the Night Child was the one who had to contend with this monster...not the Day Child, the accomplished, out-going, beautiful Marilyn that everyone knew and loved.

Not until Marilyn was fifty-three years old did she realize the horrifying truth. Her Day Child was the only person she had known herself to be, never knowing of the existence of her Night Child...all those years.

Unlike Marilyn, I was aware that I had consciously left my Intruder elsewhere. All the same, I was disassociating.

It is interesting that, before I had any symptoms of depression, I took refuge in friends, partly because women tend to be so honest with one another and I could talk about my restlessness. We all did. This was in the early seventies—a time when we knew something was amiss and we were desperately trying to identify what it was—and who we were. My friends understood my frustrations because they, too, had similar feelings. They made suggestions, we talked, and we listened. For many of them, the talks helped, but for me, the agitation persisted...and grew.

Perhaps I should have taken heed to the early signs that I now recognize were indications of mental illness. But I just didn't see them. Friends would later say there were things that should have been red flags. But how do you know the difference?

One afternoon in 1981, my friend Pam had commented, "Sue (my daughter Susan was "Sue" growing up in Pennsylvania) didn't seem too disappointed that she didn't win her match today." I concurred.

Pam's next remark was that *I* seemed to be the one who was upset, much more so than my daughter. She wondered why it was affecting me so deeply. It was just a tennis match, not a state tournament, after all. I brushed the comment aside.

Keeping my friends over the years has been challenging, especially with all my bouts with this illness coupled with the many moves we have made. Maintaining these friendships has been well worth the effort. I have carefully nurtured my relationships with others, both when in Pennsylvania and here in Colorado. Many of my best friends are relatives, my sister, Susan, being at the top of the list. As we have grown up, my sister Betsy has become very close to both Susan and me. We talk most every day, and get together frequently.

My sister relationships don't stop with Susan and Betsy, however, because I have nine sisters-in-law! I remember asking my editor if I should mention the name of my sister-in-law, Fran, in one of the Snapshots in this book and she didn't think it was necessary since it would be obvious about whom I would be talking. When she realized the number of "sisters" I have, she quickly changed her mind. So, it is with much love and deep appreciation that I thank Fran, Marion, Jonnie, Susan, Kay, Lou Ann, Sandy, Sally and Paula as well as Carol who, though not an official sister-in-law, is much more than a cousin, for the years and years of love and friendship each has so unselfishly provided.

Controlling my environment was a technique that worked well.

SNAPSHOT
State College, Pennsylvania Fall of 1979

What a God-awful day. I thought it would never end...commitments and waking up depressed are like oil and water. Hated every minute.

I put on my navy blue pants. Made of soft cotton, they are familiar, roomy. The white cotton shirt I slip over my head has a tear on the shoulder. So what? I'm not going anywhere. These are my "comfort clothes." Like old friends, they feel good.

It's quiet in the basement, cool. Everything in its place...

I refold the small, reversible afghan, carefully returning it to the back of the couch. Now the brown side is showing, and I am better.

Organization, lack of clutter, silence...all provided relief. The need for arranging became excessive and I found myself obsessing about the precise placement of things. The slant of a magazine on the coffee table, the specific coffee cup I chose, putting the right foot down on the first step...all blatant indications of obsessive compulsiveness. But that problem is preferable to being anxiety ridden.

Goal setting was automatic to me, but still a good technique to work on. Just getting up in the morning was a goal, sometimes a very difficult one to meet. Making breakfast was another. The need to fold clothes, iron (remember the days?), collect the mail...all were goals. Sound like small goals? An apt analogy is that the completion of such goals was like climbing Mt. Everest.

Sometimes two goals were accomplished by completing one task. Cleaning up the kitchen was both a chore that needed doing and a way to organize my environment and that, my friend, is implausibly satisfying when I am depressed.

Do the need for activity, goals and organization make a difference? They did for me. I would make a list...a detailed list.

1. Work on course term paper
2. Get a run in
3. Wash a load of laundry—dark clothes

Or when substitute teaching...

1. Look over lesson plans
2. Review math lesson step by step
3. Greet class at outside door today

First a morning list, then an afternoon list that was just as detailed. This was an *absolute* to get through each day.

Avoiding disappointments was a hard one to achieve. If losing a tennis match was a major disappointment, how could I cope with something earth shattering? Fortunately, I never had to. But just trying to cope with normal disappointments made my world fall apart many, many times.

"Try to put this in perspective, Ann," Gary tells me.

"Try to put it in perspective?" I think to myself. "Who is he kidding? My whole life is sorely out of perspective. What a dumb thing to say to me. Eliminate that phrase and maybe our conversation will make sense."

SNAPSHOT

We were in the living room on Ellen Avenue discussing another "major disappointment."

Dave wasn't ready for the science test.

We had crammed the night before (I had insisted because my kid can't fail, right?). But fourth grade boys would rather play baseball in the street or ride bikes to the Quick Way. The result of his procrastinating and my lack of time for drilling of scientific facts have resulted in a "D."

I am devastated...distressed beyond belief. I am panicked. His teacher will question my parenting ability. She won't like Dave any more. I am embarrassed.

"But how will he get into college?" I lament, leaping from failing an insignificant science test to total academic failure.

This neurotic banter would sometimes continue for an hour or so. This was the way it was for Gary and me...day after day after day after day! Exhausting for me, exasperating for him.

So, to protect myself from all of this anguish, I would not ask Dave or Susan how they did on tests. I would not ask about how well they played in a sport. It was too painful to risk the possibility that the results might not have been good.

I also had used a technique that I labeled "*pushing*." This is a cognitive therapy skill that works to a degree. It is difficult to perfect, and I don't think I was ever able to, but not for lack of trying.

Pushing is something that you do by yourself. It is mental activity rather than vocal. You, in essence, play dual roles while having a conversation with yourself that goes something like this:

- Positive thought – Jim (a boss) was certainly pleased with my report.

- Negative response – But I had trouble speaking intelligently and just couldn't seem to come up with appropriate words at times. I'm sure he thinks I'm a dope.

- Positive comeback – Oh, come on. He knows me too well. Everyone has that problem from time to time.

- Negative thinking – Yes, but I sounded so stupid. He probably thinks I didn't even write the report. What if he does think that? The word will get around.

- Positive remark spoken with anger – Get a grip. Don't be ridiculous... you're not even thinking straight.

In essence, you are pushing away negative thoughts with positive ones. It's difficult because immediately after a positive thought comes another negative one...one that has been waiting in the wings! But, after practicing it often, pushing becomes more effective and results in a change of thinking on many occasions.

Thinking positively is important. You probably are thinking, "Who is she kidding?" Good question. How can even the smallest bits of *positive* squeeze into the midst of so much pessimism? Well, it was not easy (an understatement).

I would often try to create a change of mood...such as listening to music (if I was able to listen to outside stimuli), researching depression at the library, or praying like mad. Anything, I would try anything and everything. Ultimately, something would click, and I would feel a bit better. You see, even a *bit* better is a tremendous relief.

Thinking a negative thought repeatedly is called *ruminating*. It is paralyzing. You think that you will be stuck with that thought forever. A feeling of hopelessness washes over me and anxiety attacks set in. It is a very out of control feeling.

If I realized I was ruminating, I would do the pushing technique. Moving from ruminating to pushing and back to ruminating would help, but it required much concentration along with a good amount of determination.

Come one, come all! The event of the moment is yet another competition of negative thoughts competing with positive ones. It's a bout between Ronnie Ruminating and Paul Pushing. Ruminating delivers a major blow. Pushing staggers. Back and forth, back and forth. What will the outcome be? Usually my competitiveness would kick in (thank God for being competitive!) and Pushing would emerge victorious. Whew! The fight would be over...but stay tuned because more will follow.

Avoiding self-absorption is important, but this is not hard for me to do. I know that I feel better when I do something for others...write a note, bake cookies or run errands. Besides, such things keep me busy, making time go by more quickly.

It also needs to be kept in mind that what may appear as self-absorption to others is simply self-preservation to those who are depressed. You really can't think beyond yourself when in despair. That's why Gary assumed so many of the parenting and errand-running responsibilities. I was too much "inside" myself and unable to function on the outside.

I admire people I see at events or in restaurants with portable oxygen tanks. If you notice, they have smiles on their faces as they enjoy what they are doing. They are making themselves available to the rest of the family...and they are happier because of taking the effort to do so. Many homebound people who are too ill to get out often volunteer by stuffing envelopes or making telephone calls for various organizations. Like them, being useful, as well as being of assistance to others, only results in a lift in self-esteem.

I truly believe that it is impossible to be happy if you never do anything for others. Think about it. Self-absorbed people, who wallow in self-pity and never reach out to others, are unable to get out from under their "Woe Is Me" blanket that covers them. I have known several such people in my lifetime, and seeing their misery and bitterness serve as an example of how unhappiness will always persist if you only consider yourself.

My determination to do what I can to create a change of mood is my way of getting away from being self-absorbing. Just looking around at my environment helps...I love cool mornings. I love sunny skies, the beginning of each season and the cooing of pigeons in the early morning. Even though it is hard to have a positive attitude when depressed, my basic nature is that of being positive. Maybe I automatically revert to it, I don't know. I do know, though, that it's not terribly difficult to see beauty, good or possibilities of what "might be." After all, each time I did something to help myself, such as go to therapy, read about my illness or make cookies for my children, I was reaching for the possibility of what "might be." In my case, at moments such as these, there was a possibility that I "*might be* happy, *might be* better, or, just maybe even find an opportunity to laugh."

Part 4

SAVORING MY LIFE

Honey,
I am sure that we can survive anything as long as we
go through it together. Our companionship, which
has grown from childhood friends into more love than
our folks or anyone else wants to realize, will be our
secret to happiness in the years to come.
We are at a stage in our lives that is filled with much
confusion, but also anticipation. We are standing at
the crossroads of life, wondering which way to go.
One thing I know, we will travel those roads together.

I love you,
Gary

(From the inside back cover of –The Wildcat,
my senior high school yearbook, 1960) Central High School

CHAPTER 25:
Looking at the World
in a Different Light

Given my "susceptibility to instability," I am inclined to lay the blame for my setbacks squarely on the many moves that we made. While "normal" people might experience all the feelings of loss that I felt, they feel them to a much lesser extent and begin to adjust far sooner than I did. It's typical to be sad, to miss the friends left behind or to cry now and then. Most people don't go into deep, lengthy depressions as I have done each time we have moved. They are able to eat and sleep, enjoy their new surroundings and see the good in the decision they made despite the fact that they sorely miss all that they left behind.

It was not this way for me. My stress reserve is lower than normal and the moves were too much with which to contend. Each move meant leaving friends and feeling that void until new friendships were made. It meant finding my way around new neighborhoods. Finding a new grocery store, a gas station and a bank was agonizing. Where do I go to get my hair cut? Where are the best places to run or play tennis? Where will I find the library, wash the car or shop for clothes? And what doctors, dentist and veterinarians are highly rated?

I must say that when I have succeeded in overcoming the struggles that this illness creates, I have always emerged a far better person. Each time my depression dissipated, I had more conviction, was more determined and knew I was capable of working through difficult situations simply because of the adversity I had conquered. All of this has resulted in looking at my world very differently.

SAVORING STABILITY

My life is constant at this time. It had been that way for nearly a decade prior to the last episode when we lived in Mississippi in 2000. It took two years to recover from that last bout, but I have not experienced any symptoms since then. We have stability in our lives once again...Gary and I are both content with our work, we live near our children and grandchildren and know that we will never uproot ourselves again.

While my extended and immediate families have always been important to me, they are now cherished. Each day is wonderful, far richer than any day was before depression entered my life. I once thought that I knew what happiness was...now happiness has taken on a much deeper meaning.

I do know it's been a very gradual climb up the precipice of depression to arrive at the pinnacle. Looking back, even that mountainous climb did have beauty and joy. Although in this book I have focused primarily on the bad times, so many times were good...

SNAPSHOT
Denver, Colorado April 1995

I awaken seconds before the loud sound. My mind goes through the usual procedure...why is the alarm ringing? What day is it? The answers to each of these racing thoughts tumble across my mind almost as quickly as I am thinking them.

It's Friday...tomorrow I can sleep in, get things accomplished around the house, run a few errands, maybe a quiet dinner with Gary Saturday night.

As I drive the eight miles to school, I think through my schedule. I love Fridays in particular because we don't follow our regular routine. It's kind of a catch-up day, culminated by an activity time of thirty minutes for my students who have had a good week. They love this, and it serves as an incentive for them to do their best.

The day is sunny and, as I travel west, I notice the mountains in the distance. They are snow-capped, majestic, shades of blues and purples. I feel fortunate to travel this route each day, driving toward the Colorado Rockies.

I love waking up each day knowing that I am no longer depressed, that I am able to enjoy each moment. I no longer take happiness for granted; rather, I revel in it.

I love what I do, where I live…the town, the neighborhood, and our house. I love being so close to family, taking part in family activities and celebrations. I love the fact that Susan and Dave live in Denver, and are an integral part of our lives.

I turn off Hampden as I approach Broadway to travel several blocks northward before I reach my school. Pulling up to the curb I notice the beauty of the day. Stepping into my classroom, I am aware of the cleanliness, the familiar smell, and the organization in which I left it. I put my school bag down, write the date on the chalkboard and prepare for the day. I take each small chair off the desks, placing them where they belong.

My colleagues walk up the hall to grab cups of coffee, check messages and mailboxes, calling out greetings to one another as well as to me. I answer. The bell sounds at 8:15 and I walk to the outside door to meet my class.

Smiles greet me as I push open the door, touching each of them lightly as they walk past. These are the best kids in the world. Some of them move into me, giving me an abbreviated hug as they walk by.

Marie is crying. She has on a jump suit that she claims has prompted a couple of the boys to call her a hippie. I put my arm around her as we approach the classroom.

Marie is a bright, creative child, gifted in writing and full of personality. Her creativeness lends itself to her sensitivity.

"Well," I tell her with a smile, "You do look somewhat like a hippie, but a very cute hippie!"

She laughs through her tears. The crisis is over.

> Many of the children are talking, sharing what they brought for afternoon Activity Time, and making plans with one another. Everyone settles into his or her seat, busily copying the daily activity from the board into their reading journal.
>
> I sit on the small desk at the front of the room and take attendance and lunch count. Another school day has begun... and I am happy.

In looking back, I look forward. My life is far richer having lived through the horrific lows that depression creates. When I am in the middle of the darkness, I know that it will pass. Waiting is *always* difficult, especially since time goes too slowly when depression is present. But I know that my life eventually will be happy again so I do everything I can think of to see that I can reach the top of that mountain.

I COUNT MY BLESSINGS

I know that I have a wonderful life in my favor. I know that once depression leaves, my world is a stable one. For many people, this is not the case. They often emerge to once again face a dysfunctional family, unemployment or a life alone. When there is nothing hopeful beyond the hopelessness, I can see why many believe it's not worth the tremendous effort it takes to survive the agony of this illness.

But there are always reasons for a person to live. Children depend on those who teach, and the bonds you develop with coworkers, no matter where you work, often affect those left behind much more than can be predicted.

Think about your life in general, a day in your life in particular. Who are the people you enjoy seeing? Perhaps it's people you see once a week at church, a neighbor or a personal friend. Suicide affects those who remain. I truly believe that each one of us is much more important to those with whom we interact than we think we are. Remember, this decision is not just about you...it really isn't.

LESSONS LEARNED

I learned that little things are not important. They are perhaps a disappointment with which to contend—a part of what life is all about.

It is easy to love now, to exult in the good days and value life more passionately.

Depression has provided me much deeper insight into myself and what I am all about as a person. I know that I am stronger, kinder, and even more tolerant that I was before. I have more compassion and am more willing to reach out to others when they need comfort or assistance. Sunny days are brighter, smiles sweeter and life is far more precious.

I have learned that I am responsible for my happiness, even though I often have no control over it. I know that I cannot live through the happiness of others, but must experience it myself to be happy.

The day I learned and accepted that depression would probably come and go my entire life was a breakthrough in my recovery. Knowing that it would never disappear forever was a pragmatic realization that has enabled me to be prepared for future incidences.

I have learned that life is too short to live it the way others think you should rather than the way you want to live it. As a young mother I would often find myself agreeing to do something that I had no desire to do. Someone would recruit me for some task, and I would reluctantly agree knowing full well that I just should have refused. While 'no' seems to be a difficult word for many people, being depressed was a catalyst to my using it often. Since good days are far fewer, I need to make the best of them. I want to spend my time the way I want to spend it so I guard it carefully. This is one area of my life where I experience no guilt being selfish.

Not long ago, my daughter Susan remarked about how quickly time passes and asked me if it bothered me. I told her that I have never been happier. Each day is a gift, something I enjoy from the time I awaken until the light is turned out at night. This wasn't true for many, many years. In the days ahead, I may find myself in the midst of yet another depression. Until that happens, I luxuriate in the happiness that surrounds me, tackling problems rationally, knowing that there will always be bumps as we travel along life's road.

ON BEING A MOTHER

There was only one part of my life that was never difficult, and in which the Old Ann has always existed, and that was the part of being a mother. I have always loved being a mother. I have always known that I am a great mother, the kind who makes play dough with the kids, who bakes and takes them to petting zoos. We read books twice a day, something I looked forward to as much as they did.

We went on picnics to the park; we went to the pool on the Penn State campus and we climbed mountains. I encouraged them to jump in puddles and to roll in the mud, to make snow angels and to set up lemonade stands.

Each time they would wrap their arms around my neck and tell me that they loved me, my pain lessened a little, and I knew that I *had* to endure it...for them and for their father. I'm certain that many people who commit suicide had no reason to stay in the horrific place that depression creates. I also know that many of them sadly do not have the resolve to endure depression's pain, and I can well understand because it was very hard for me to make the decision "to stay" time and time again. But even though I was determined, I don't know how I managed because it is hard to go against what you desperately want, particularly hard when dealing with this illness. Determination, love for your family and commitment to yourself are sometimes not enough. Fortunately they have been for me.

As my kids were growing up, their mom was the mom they had always known. She was the old Ann. They never knew the other Ann because I never introduced them to that unwelcome intruder. She would have frightened them and caused their lives to change direction so I hid her from them. My instincts as a mother were far too strong for her to intrude; she was never victorious in penetrating this part of my life.

AFTERTHOUGHTS:
Reflecting Back While Looking Forward

Writing this book has helped me see life a lot more clearly. Some things have become apparent for the first time. It is like I am a schoolgirl again and have a new teacher. In a sense this book has been a catharsis for the tremendous obstacles I have overcome—a release of all the remnants of anguish remaining in my head. I highly recommend writing...books, journals or even just letters to a friend.

WHERE TO GO FROM HERE

It has been over seven years since the time I experienced my last major depression, I have been mentally healthy for five years. Where do I go from here? What precautions can I take that might ward off a future bout? Will the depression return?

I have no way of predicting its revisit, but I now know specific precautions to take. I know that we will never move again. It is important for my well being that I remain in the familiarity of my house, my community and, most imperative, my children and grandchildren. Given the fact that much of what we do here revolves around our children, I must be in the midst of all of it.

Exercising, eating right and getting enough sleep are ways I can help myself. Stress avoidance is to my advantage because it means that my life is calmer, more enjoyable.

I will continue to take my medication and to see Dr. Bell at least twice a year. In this way, I will be able to maintain my health and be proactive to any concerns that might develop into something larger if they are not addressed. I am a huge advocate of both because it is due to both that I have been able to bring my life back into focus so many times. All the years I have spent dealing with the many symptoms of this terrible affliction has resulted in my becoming an "expert" on my personal needs. I have never pretended to know what others need. I can only recommend and discuss how I helped myself. It is by reading, listening and being aware of what we can do that will improve our quality of life that we are able to do so. Know that overcoming depression is possible.

SNAPSHOT
Denver, Colorado September 26, 2006

I have given much thought to what loved ones can do to prevent those who experience depression from committing suicide. Can we really stop someone from ending his/her life? What might we do that will change the minds of those in terrible mental pain? Is our "after the fact" guilt justified?

She was one of the students I most remember. Always smiling, bright and eager to learn, everyone loved her...peers and teachers alike. An asset to any class, I was fortunate that she was in mine. Exuding self-confidence, along with humility, she was everything you would hope that a child could be...so "together."

Recently, she committed suicide. Her mother spoke at the memorial, asking that the peers of her daughter think twice about drinking, about doing drugs. She said that her daughter equated her self-worth with popularity and that her quest for the friends she needed had gotten in the way of her direction. She had lost her way, and, regrettably, was unable to find her way back.

I wanted to tell her mother, "Don't blame yourself," because I know that our decisions are often made regardless of what others want for us.

I wanted to tell her mother, "You could never have prevented this," because I know this to be true.

I wanted to tell her mother, "She did this because she loved you, because she truly believed that she was a burden that had gotten in the way of your happiness," because the thinking of those who suffer this illness is dreadfully skewed.

But I didn't tell her any of that. I told her to call me, that I had years of struggles of my own and could maybe...just maybe...help her to understand what might have gone on in the mind of her daughter.

RESOURCES:
How Others Can Help

To help those family members and friends provide support to loved ones who experience the many symptoms of depression, I want to offer these suggestions. Before you begin reading this section, the most important thing to understand is that you can't understand. It simply is not possible. This should not stop you from playing a key role because it is necessary that you give whatever support you are able to give.

There is no magic formula. It is difficult to know how to help because the needs of each individual are different. In addition, what provides comfort at any given time may not have the same effect at another time. With this in mind, I can only offer advice from a personal perspective, explaining the many ways that others were able to provide help for me.

A TRIBUTE TO MY SPOUSE

Many times when I was not able to talk, I would just sit on the couch or lie on my bed, but Gary would often be there with me. He would talk to me and I would give non-verbal responses...nods, smiles or touches. He would hold me, sometimes for long periods of time; maybe nothing was said, but at least we were together and this meant more to me than I have ever been able to convey to him. Many days I couldn't wait until he walked in the door after work. He tried so hard. He was always there for me and he was my security.

Yet, even Gary, who got as close and intimate with depression as you can get, couldn't always know what to do.

During the years that we were raising our children, there were many, many times when Gary had to take over most of the parental responsibility; this might be for days at a time, a couple of months or, sometimes, even longer because I had so much difficulty just helping myself get through each day. He would go to the store, drive Susan and Dave where they needed to go and run necessary errands. This was asking a lot from him since he had a full time job as well, but he never complained. He was always willing to do whatever needed to be done. So this enabled me to manage only my part of my life rather than the needs of the entire family. It bothered me immensely, knowing that I was not giving the family much of myself, but his commitment to all of us greatly lessened my guilt.

I was always a part of the family even while Gary was making decisions. We attempted to have as normal a family life as was possible, and I know that we achieved this goal. It gave our children continuity in their daily routine and the "normal" childhood I desperately wanted for them.

Just having someone there lets those who are suffering know that you care. They may not be able to "feel" the care than you communicate, but they *know*. Those in deep depression are incapable of feeling; this is certainly the way it is for me. Just intellectually being aware that those who love me demonstrate it in one way or another...a phone call, a card, or a smile...is imperative.

So, to all spouses, significant others and close friends: #1, be available.

TALK ABOUT SUICIDE...OFTEN

This is the word that Gary and I never mentioned, but I now strongly believe that it is critical that this subject be *continually* addressed when depression is present. I used to believe that if the word were never articulated, the person who was depressed would not consider this option. This belief could not be further from the truth.

Severe depression and suicidal thoughts go hand in hand. When I was in my dark days, I thought about suicide most of the time. Not talking about it did nothing to erase it from my mind. What a relief it would have provided! Family members and close friends need to address this, thereby allowing their loved ones the opportunity to discuss the implications fully.

It should be kept in mind, though, that during the seventies and eighties the fact that we never uttered the word was understandable. Anything having to do with mental problems was strictly taboo. But even though the word was never verbalized, what we both said clearly communicated that the subject was a major part of our thinking. I knew that Gary was aware of my thinking just as he knew how tempting suicide was for me. A typical conversation would be along these lines:

"I know you will feel better once you see Sandy. Going to him always improves your mood."

"But I don't want to go. I just want to stay here because I can't function at all. I am more depressed now than I have been in weeks. I don't think I can do this."

"Look at me. Promise me, Ann; promise me that you will never do anything to yourself. I would never forgive myself, and the repercussions for the kids would be terrible."

I would nod, and I would dismiss the temptation because the subject had been broached even though the word had not been mentioned. I got the message, but I do believe that it would have been better if we had said the word. The message would have been more emphatic if we had.

Years later, both Susan and Dave were bluntly honest with me. They mentioned the word suicide, and made me promise not to commit it. It was then that I realized how much more powerful the plea is when that word is spoken. I also realized that I could not kill myself...no matter the temptation.

So, if someone you know who is severely depressed tells you they have never thought about suicide, don't believe it for a minute. There is no way that it does not enter the minds of those who suffer deeply from this illness. I would assume one of two things...either the person is not being honest or he or she isn't severely depressed.

Family members left behind often make the comment that, although their loved one had been despondent, he or she had seemed so happy of late. I was happy too when I decided to commit suicide because I knew that my suffering would soon end. I am certain that this is the reason for such behavior changes in many who suffer from depression.

ACKNOWLEDGE THE PAIN AND LEARN ABOUT IT

The last thing that I want to hear from someone is that I "just need to cheer up" and that I have much to live for, so many advantages, etc. All of this is irrelevant and makes no sense when I am depressed. I would cheer up if I could! Depression isn't something I choose to be; it cannot be turned off at will.

I will never forget the person who knew about my struggles telling me that when she went through her divorce she just told herself that she wasn't going to get depressed, so she didn't! It was an insensitive comment because it inferred that I "allowed" my depression. I realized how naïve her remark was. It was also apparent that she had never experienced depression.

If anyone ever tells you that they "think" they were once depressed, or that they "might have" been depressed, be assured that they have not been. If you are depressed, you know it without a doubt.

I am well aware that I make my family feel helpless and that I become extremely dependent upon them. The guilt continues to grow with each realization that I am creating unhappiness and frustration in others. It's aggravating to not be able to alleviate the pain of someone you love, but it's not always possible to do this.

Just knowing that others *try* to understand is a tremendous help to me. It's important to validate the feelings of those who have this illness. Gary has watched me suffer incredible pain. He has read every book that was recommended by my therapists. I know that he understands depression as well as anyone can be expected to understand it not having ever experienced it.

SUSAN: "The main memory I have in dealing with my mother's most intense bouts of depression is repeatedly having the same discussions with her. Over and over again I would try to build her up, to reassure her and talk her out of her paranoid state. These discussions were typically pep talks or strategizing to help her cope and get through her day.

"It would be weeks at a time that I would find myself saying the exact same thing to try to comfort/reassure her. This patient and loving approach is something I tried hard to maintain, and I fully appreciated what my dad had always provided for my mom all these years.

"The continual support you give to someone who is depressed is absolutely draining but so necessary. Even as an adult and fully appreciating the disease, I still found myself at a loss as to how to help. I knew words would never talk her out of her mood or result in her "snapping out of it," but it was necessary to continually boost her up to sustain her ability to function and ultimately avoid suicide. People dealing with a loved one's depression truly need to be equipped with a thorough understanding of the illness and the maturity to be supportive time and time again.

"Family members need to be in constant communication and be a supportive team for one another as this time is exhausting, frustrating and, yes, it can be scary. Teenagers should be made aware of the diagnosis and the corresponding symptoms so they can better understand his or her parent's behavior, which can range from depressed, paranoid and non-functional to overly happy and erratic.

These mood changes and/or manifestations of their condition can be confusing and misunderstood.

"For instance, many times my mom was distant and unresponsive. A young adult might confuse this for not caring or loving them. Conversely, my mom demonstrated huge swings of emotions. Some days she could barely converse and other days she would be laughing loudly and talking non-stop. For anyone unfamiliar with depression the latter behavior could seem like her depression had passed, but within hours she could cycle back to a non-communicative state. So by becoming well-informed, you may be more tolerant of the situation and less likely to internalize things."

INTERACT WITH DIGNITY AND RESPECT

When interacting with family members who are depressed, treat them with dignity and respect. Talk to them as adults on your level rather than someone who should be coddled or discounted. It's demeaning to do otherwise. Ask their opinions, tell them about your day; treat them as you did before they experienced this illness. When I am having bad days, I maintain interaction with all family members, asking my kids how their days were and trying to keep our lives as normal as possible. I want to be a part of their reality of life.

Since neither of my children, as youngsters, was cognizant of my problems, life was as normal as it could have been and this, I believe, made it easier for me to cope. Being around them provided the opportunity for me to be the mom I had always been, knowing that they were never being condescending. They were able to express their true feelings and frustrations rather than attempt to cover them up. And while I sometimes did not want to hear about their unhappiness, I knew that it was this was very much a part of normal living. I felt needed when I would comfort them and discuss their problems with them. They would run off feeling much better, and I would be grateful, not only that they had come to me, but that I had allowed them to do so.

DAVE: "These are my thoughts for support persons, especially the children of a depressed parent. Be very supportive. Learn as much as you can about the illness your spouse or parent is dealing with. Be very patient and empathetic. No matter how difficult things are for you, you have no way of comprehending how challenging life is for your loved one. His or her world is quite different from the one you are living in.

"Go to a therapist so that you can gain a better understanding of the illness as well as the medication that is being prescribed. Learn about the side effects of the medication and how they might affect the behavior of your loved one.

"For me, I wish I could have understood what my mother was going through. I realize that my parents wanted to shelter me, but this was an issue that was too big for all of us. Had I known the depths of my mom's illness, I would have been able to help. I think that deep down part of my struggles with all the moves were due to the fact that I knew something was wrong, but kept being told that everything was fine. I knew that it wasn't.

"My dad did an amazing job of keeping everything together. His unrelenting love and compassion is what got us through all of this.

UNDERSTAND THE DESIRE FOR PRIVACY

Many of us who are depressed want solitude. This reduces the stress that comes with the uncertainty that is created when others are present. I like people, but I often cannot cope with others around and have to do what is best for me. Uncertainty and activity can create anxiety. It is important that family members and friends understand that such behavior is not to be taken as personal rejection.

There were many times when I was very reluctant to attend social events only to discover that my mood would improve once I was there. Other times, however, the depression remained, so it was hard for Gary to know just how far to push me to go. I can't predict how I will react so it is understandable that he would not be able to either. In many instances, though, I was so distressed that I didn't even consider leaving home, and he respected this. Sometimes I was able to persuade him to go alone, but he usually opted to stay home with me.

EXPECT READJUSTMENT AMONG FAMILY MEMBERS

Once I began to recover and gain back confidence, I felt more comfortable making decisions. I slowly resumed my role as wife and mother, but I discovered that, because Gary had been doing so much, it was difficult to readjust. It was hard for both of us. I found myself taking exception to his intrusion and often disagreed with his choices. Conversely, he resented my objection to his parenting. I disagreed with the discipline approach he took with Dave and insisted on taking a different approach in the future. Understandably, this created problems. I am sure Dave can attest to this.

It wasn't that Gary didn't want me to return to my former roles. He was, in fact, grateful that I felt well enough to do so, but it was a power struggle for quite some time. He wasn't used to me interfering, let alone objecting to his decisions. I understood his reluctance. It was two-fold...he was reluctant to give up his control and, at the same time, it was hard for him to trust my decisions. Eventually, we were both able to feel comfortable again, and family life returned to what it had been before depression entered our lives.

With each depression came more adjustments, and each differed from the others. Because symptoms are so varied and their intensity changes, my role was different, Gary's role was different and what we needed from one another changed as well. This is not easy. It is actually quite complicated. Things go along well, then the depression reappears, we have to readjust and never can predict how long all of this will take.

Length and intensity are not considerations because you don't think ahead. You just take one day at a time because that's all you can handle. You adjust and readjust as needed, trying to do your best for the entire family.

GARY: "As the years passed, I came to understand that more important than anything else, what Ann needed was unrelenting support. To the extent possible, we walked through this depression together. Today, some thirty-plus years after it all began, Ann's life is back to normal. She knows that depression is always lurking in the background. She knows that she will spend the rest of her life on medication, getting counseling and, undoubtedly, periodically dealing with bouts of depression. But we have survived all the other bouts and have emerged stronger and closer than ever. We are still best friends, better than ever lovers, once again full partners in life. Moreover, Ann is a self-assured, competent, fulfilled person, full of love for life and all the opportunities it presents. She serves as proof to all that it is possible to live with depression."

EPILOGUE:
On Being Grammy

What a satisfying feeling! Not only have I completed a book...I have a publisher who believes in its content. And I still have time for my other passion—my grandchildren. I love being with them, and I am with them often. Susan has her own business that takes her to conferences in different parts of the country throughout the year. When possible, her husband John accompanies her because she needs help with selling her products and making presentations.

Before they took the step to go to another level with the business, John and Susan sat down with Gary and me to ask if we would be willing to watch the children during the times they are away. Of course we jumped at the opportunity, knowing how we enjoy being with the children, but also because we want to do what we can to help support Susan's professional goals.

Surprising Susan for their fifteenth anniversary/fortieth birthday celebration, John arranged a week in Hawaii. Before plans were made, he questioned my willingness and availability, so I found myself with all three cherubs last week (September 2006).

A VERY INTERESTING WEEK

Our days went along this line:

Alarm rings at 6:00...make coffee, dress and apply makeup since it may be the only chance I have for some time. Let Chloe, our dog, out, let Chloe in, delay feeding Chloe since Max wants to do it so that he can earn $1.00 for the week.

Kids are awakened at 6:50...they dress in outfits laid out for them the night before, eat breakfast, brush teeth and hair, gather backpacks and sweaters in time to walk several blocks with three of the neighborhood kids who live on the cull de sac.

7:45 – I look around at a very messy kitchen that had been completely cleaned the night before. Left over biscuits, jelly dripped on the countertop and honey on knives, half-filled juice glasses and fruit that is beginning to darken stand awry amidst mixing bowl and opened Bisquick box.

I sigh and pour another cup of coffee.

I hear movement on the stairs, and a tousled head peeks around the corner.

"It must be that little mouse." I say out loud to the small boy who lately pretends he is a mouse.

Ben laughs as I grab him up in my arms. "Now," I say, "What do you want for breakfast"?

Quickly clean up kitchen, straighten up bedrooms, and pull quilts over the top of beds. Ben and I take off for my house where I can write for a couple of hours while he occupies himself with puzzles and cars. I make the bed for Gary, who has left it as is. Throwing in a load of wash, I make a few quick phone calls. Then I sit down at the computer.

Answer phone, continue with laundry, sit down and write some more... more of the same until I discover a weight on my back. Ben, with arms draped around my neck, stands behind me as I am typing while sitting on the desk chair. "Um," I think. "Must be time to go..."

Save file, call dog and the three of us pile into the car to head for Susan's house.

Once there, Ollie arrives at the door asking if Ben can play. I let him in and they head upstairs where I know they will soon create yet another mess. Next thing I know, Morgan and Garret are there as well, the four preschoolers playing together on the bedroom floor. Phone rings and Ollie's mother inquires if we have seen him. I assure her all is well, and we decide to meet the kids at the pool after school.

I give my daughter-in-law, Kelly, a quick call to see if she and Morgan, my fourth cherub, want to meet us later. Not too many hot days left, swimming will be fun.

The neighborhood pool area teems with kids. Kids doing homework on the pavement dressed in bathing suits, kids in the pool, kids arriving with backpacks in hand. Mine help themselves to granola bars and lemonade that Julie (Ollie's mom) and I have brought along, change and head for the water.

I sit with young mothers I know as we discuss kids, teachers and the end of summer. Ben and several other little ones play in the baby pool while Anna and Max climb the high dive, splash in the water and swim to the side. Hoisting themselves out, they continue with more of the same.

"They are swimming much better," I think to myself. "Now Ben needs to learn." I think of him running straight into the deep end after Max and Anna have done the same a few weeks earlier. "Watch them every minute, every minute, every minute," I say, repeating the pool mantra.

Back home, kids change, I argue with Max to do his homework, listen to Anna telling about her day while Ben works more puzzles. Phone rings, Max leaves for soccer practice while I prepare dinner.

Rest of the school days are the same except that by Friday morning I am almost unable to get out of bed. TGIF! I think.

Ongoing frustrations for the week are small, but annoying:

- Anna makes a fuss when I attempt to comb her hair before school. (You would think I was killing her!) I send her across the cull de sac one morning telling her to tell Camille (mother of six) to do it for her. I tell her that it looks great when she returns. "It's just a pony tail, Grammy." I guess it is just a pony tail, but it doesn't look at all like the ones I have tried to make while struggling with a wiggling six year old each morning.

- Mr. Procrastinator, Max, has great reasons for delaying the homework-time each day...quite creative, it turns out. His arguments fail. I win.

- Bedtime is a chore...for all of us. Books are read to Anna and Ben as Max reads to himself. At long last, all are sleeping and I read until I do the same only to awaken later with three other people sound asleep in bed with me.

- Neighborhood kids (bless them) are in and out, in and out all week. You can find them in any room, sometimes without any of the home occupants around.

In addition to all the usual responsibilities, I attend Back to School Nights for all three...two on Wednesday night and one on Thursday evening. Soccer practice for Anna is Thursday afternoon. She tries to get away with wearing sandals, but I insist she go in tennis shoes. She wants to ride her bike down and back, so I follow her each way.

Friday night we meet Dave, Kelly and four-year-old Morgan for pizza. As I sit looking around the table, I treasure the moment, and savor the realization that I feel so good. Another thought goes through my mind: I might have missed all this if I had done what I so wanted to do so many times. I would have missed those hair fights, homework arguments, early mornings and crowded beds. I would have not been "Grammy" to these four children I so cherish.

* * *

We now have a fifth grandchild to love, the baby sister that Morgan has so wanted and a new cousin for Max, Anna and Ben.

Nina arrived two weeks early, in March rather than April, just as was true of her father's arrival thirty-seven years prior.

"What's her name?" Anna asks her Aunt Kelly as we all crowd around to catch of peek at this very new baby.

"Her name is Nina," Kelly responds.

Nina, I think. What a beautiful name. Nina.

"And what is her middle name?" Anna continues.

"Her middle name is Ann. Her name is Nina Ann," Kelly answers.

I suddenly remember all those moments of darkness and despair; all of the times I so desperately wanted to commit suicide. I remember the hundreds of times I had to keep reminding myself that I would get through the pain even though I was convinced that each time was the one time that the pain would never leave. And, then I look around at this wonderful family of mine, so full of happiness and I know that today would have been very different if I had not lived through all of that pain. Nina Ann seems to be looking at all of us as her mother gently holds her for all to see...and I silently begin to cry...

Selected Bibliography

BOOKS:

Berne, Eric, M.D. *Games People Play: The basic handbook of transactional analysis*. New York: Ballantine Books, 1964.

Burns, David D., M.D. *Feeling Good: The New Mood Therapy*. New York: Avon Books, 1980.

Duke, Patty and Hochman, Gloria. *A Brilliant Madness: Living With Manic Depressive Illness*. New York: Bantam Books, 1992.

Emery, Gary PhD *A New Beginning: How You Can Change Your Life Through Cognitive Therapy*. New York: Touchstone, 1981.

Fieve, Ronald, M.D. *Moodswings: Dr. Fieve on Depression*. New York: Bantam Books, 1989.

Gibran, Kahlil. *The Prophet*. New York: Alfred A. Knopf, Inc. 1923

Gold, Mark S., M.D. *The Good News About Depression: Cures and Treatments in the New Age of Psychiatry*. New York: Bantam Books, 1995.

Harris, Thomas A., M.D. *I'm OK-You're OK*. New York: Harper Collins Publishers, Inc., 1967.

James, Muriel & Jongeward, Dorothy. *Born to Win: Transactional Analysis With Gestalt Experiments*. Philippines: Addison-Wesley Publishing Company, Inc., 1971.

Selected Bibliography

Jamison, Kay Redfield. *An Unquiet Mind: A Memoir of Moods and Madness.* New York: Vintage Books, 1995.

Lindbergh, Anne Morrow. *Gift From the Sea.* New York: Pantheon Books, 1955.

McGrath, Ellen Ph.D. *When Feeling Bad Is Good.* New York: Henry Holt & Company, 1992.

Mornin, Edward and Lorna. *Saints: A Visual Guide.* London: Frances Lincoln Limited, 2006.

Nasar, Sylvia. *A Beautiful Mind: A Biography of John Forbes Nash, Jr.* New York: Simon & Schuster, 1998.

Pauley, Jane. *Skywriting: A Life Out of the Blue.* New York: Random House, 2004.

Peck, M. Scott, M.D. *The Road Less Traveled: A New Psychology of Love, Traditional Values and Spiritual Growth.* New York: Simon & Schuster, Inc., 1978.

Perry, Patrick. *"Mike Wallace: Speaking Out On Depression."* The Saturday Evening Post, October 31, 2006.

Styron, William. *Darkness Visible: A Memoir of Madness.* New York: Vintage Books, 1990.

Thorne, Julia. *You Are Not Alone: Words of Experience and Hope for the Journey Through Depression.* New York: Harper Perennial, 1993.

Van Derbur, Marilyn. *Miss America By Day: Lessons Learned from Ultimate Betrayals and Unconditional Love.* Denver: Oak Hill Ridge Press, 2004.

WEB SITES:

www.nih.gov
National Institute of Health is the nation's medical research agency. Their website includes comprehensive information on health-related issues, research pursuits and findings. Research articles are available on all health issues, with links to more specific topics one might want to research.

www.medlineplus.gov
Supported by both the National Library of Medicine and the National Institutes of Health, Medline plus contains comprehensive information about health topics. Particularly helpful is the link on drug information that provides information on drug uses, side effects and contraindications.

www.webmd.com
A useful health website when seeking information about health related issues, including drug, supplement and herbal treatments.

ABOUT THE AUTHOR

Ann Kochenberger is an author and an educator. She worked at Penn State University in the areas of research and writing before she taught at the elementary and secondary levels. An avid reader and exercise enthusiast, Ann loves traveling and spending time with family, friends and her five grandchildren. The author of several published articles, *Out of Focus...Again* is her first book. She lives in Denver, Colorado with her husband Gary.